WINNING
MINDS

ROS JAY

WINNING MINDS

THE ULTIMATE BOOK OF INSPIRATIONAL BUSINESS LEADERS

CAPSTONE

The right of Ros Jay to be identified as the author of this work has been asserted in accordance with the Copyright, Designs and Patents Act 1988

First published 2001 by
Capstone Publishing Limited (a Wiley company)
8 Newtec Place
Magdalen Road
Oxford OX4 1RE
United Kingdom
http://www.capstone.co.uk

British Library Cataloguing in Publication Data
A CIP catalogue record for this book is available from the British Library

ISBN 1-84112-128-2

Typeset in 10.5/13 pt Plantin by
Sparks Computer Solutions Ltd, Oxford
http://www.sparks.co.uk
Printed and bound by
T.J. International Ltd, Padstow, Cornwall

This book is printed on acid-free paper

Substantial discounts on bulk quantities of Capstone books are available to corporations, professional associations and other organisations. For details telephone Capstone Publishing on (+44-1865-798623), fax (+44-1865-240941) or email (info@wiley-capstone.co.uk).

CONTENTS

ACKNOWLEDGEMENTS

I would like to thank everyone who has helped with material for this book, in particular the Boots Company Archive, The John Lewis Partnership, Marks and Spencer plc, J Sainsbury plc, and Andrew Alsbury.

INTRODUCTION

When I was about ten years old I had a school book about maths. The introduction explained that when we are young we ask big, simple questions: why is the sky blue? Why is water wet? Why do trees have leaves? As we grow older, we ask more detailed and complex questions. But some people go on asking the big, simple questions. We call these people Great Scientists.

It's the same in the world of business. Most of us spend our working lives on details, in small parts of the organisation and on short-term projects. Which is fine, but the management high-flyers – the future leaders – are the ones who never lose sight of the abiding principles, the wider picture and the ultimate objectives of their organisation.

The household names, the legends, are very different from each other, but all of them grasped and never let go of the great simplicities. Their organisations have developed a mass of complex operations, but the leader's mind is focused on the simple, underlying purpose and principles. This is what is often meant by 'vision'.

Looking at the lives and careers of great business leaders and visionaries is not only fascinating in itself, but is also an invaluable counterpoint to the focus on small operational details that inevitably make up most of our working lives. It makes us think about the few great simplicities behind the myriad small complexities of our own job.

I make no apology for the fact that the choice of leaders in this book is partly subjective. It has to be. There are ten or a dozen names that it would be ludicrous to leave out – names like Henry Ford, Alfred Sloan, Bill Gates, Jack Welch – but after that there are probably a couple of hundred names that you could justify including. My choice has been made deliberately to include a wide range of personalities, industries and historical span, and to cover people who succeeded as a result of different skills – financial acumen, brand building, organisational skills, salesmanship, innovative design. Something, in other words, to inspire all of us whatever our own personal strengths and interests.

This book is subtitled *The Ultimate Book of Inspirational Business Leaders*. So what does inspirational mean? Literally, of course, it means that it causes you to draw breath. It's true that the achievements of some of the people in this book are quite breathtaking. Henry Ford, for example, who virtually invented modern industry. Or Robert Woodruff, who tried his best to avoid working for Coca-Cola, but eventually turned it into the world's most recognisable brand almost in spite of himself.

But in the context of this book, I have taken the word inspirational to mean that all these people have the ability to inspire ordinary people like us to become as extraordinary as them. And the reason is that when you come to look at them, you realise that these are just ordinary people too. They all had something going for them, but they all had gaps in their abilities too. If you list all the qualities and skills that go towards making people successful business leaders, you won't find a single winner with every one of them.

And that's inspiring, because that counts us in too. We're all like that – plenty of strengths but useless at finance maybe, or hopeless with people. The thing that makes these guys the winners they are is that they knew how to cover for the gaps in their abilities. And that's what makes them so fascinating to learn about. William Lyons, who founded Jaguar cars, didn't actually know how to design an engine. Harold Geneen of ITT was hardly a born salesman. William Randolph Hearst was no diplomat. Thomas Edison was almost completely deaf, for crying out loud. But it didn't stop any of them.

What does it take?

You might not have to have every quality of leadership to succeed, but obviously you need some of them. The winners in this book were winners because – among other things – they had at least one really strong point. Edwin Land was an inspired inventor, Alfred Sloan knew how to organise a massive corporation, Estée Lauder could sell dirt to a beggar (though I doubt she'd have wanted to). So what are the ingredients of successful leadership?

They seem to fall into two categories – natural talents, and business principles. The three most significant natural talents you'll find among the pages of this book seem to be charisma, intuition and self-confidence. Many of the people who have made it into this book undoubtedly have charisma in bucketloads: Sam Walton, Herb Kellaway, Jack Welch, Akio Morita. But hang on, some of the leaders in this book have nothing you could describe, however generously, as charisma. There's Harold Geneen of ITT, for example, or Steve Case of AOL.

And the same goes for business intuition. Some people can scent a trend years ahead of everyone else. Charles Merrill was the first to see the Wall Street Crash of 1929 coming, and one of the few to get out in time. Henry Ford just *knew* that there was a mass market waiting for his Model T car. Sam Walton saw that the future of retailing lay in out-of-town stores. And Bill Gates famously predicted a computer on every desk and in every home when other people just thought he was nuts. But plenty of them made mistakes. Lord Reith didn't see any future in television. Ray Kroc may have struck it rich with McDonald's, but only after he'd spent 17 years making a meagre living flogging mixing machines that he misguidedly believed would make him his fortune.

The only universal quality you seem to find among the leaders in this selection is self-confidence. Not necessarily big, brash self-confidence, mind. Some of these leaders are quiet and self-effacing. At least two of them stammer. But all of them have the confidence to make unpopular decisions, to go in the opposite direction from the herd, and to take gambles (although some take wild pot shots while others go for carefully calculated risks). It's a self-confidence which might not be obvious on casual acquaintance, but which is evident from the way they run their businesses.

The business principles you need to follow in order to succeed are a different matter. You should be able to learn them. And in the pages that follow you'll see how brilliantly these inspirational leaders have applied them. But you'll still find that many of these people not only got by without following all these principles, but actually built huge businesses despite the omission.

There are eight core business principles that seem overwhelmingly (though not universally) to have guided the leaders in this book:

1   Put your employees first (Richard Branson, William Hesketh Lever and David Packard are prime examples of this).
2   Look after your customers (Sam Walton and Herb Kelleher are hard to beat at this one).
3   Hire the best people (Bill Gates and David Ogilvy can teach us a thing or two here).
4   Have a clear vision – and communicate it throughout the company (Robert Woodruff had such clear focus for Coca-Cola he resisted diversifying for decades).

5   Keep moving (Thomas J. Watson reckoned it was better, and faster, to solve a problem wrong than not to do anything about it at all).
6   Use anyone's ideas so long as they're good (Jack Welch is probably the world leader at this – he didn't just do it, he was proud of it).
7   Be committed to your work (Spedan Lewis gave up his life to the partnership at John Lewis, and although he had a full lifestyle outside IBM, Thomas Watson Jr still put one hundred per cent into the organisation).
8   Do what you believe in (as Anita Roddick did at the Body Shop, or Edwin Land at Polaroid).

Having said all that, you also need to find an organisation to lead that needs those skills which you possess. Not any leader can lead any organisation, or at least not to the same level of success. Can you imagine putting Anita Roddick in charge of Ford Motors? Or Alfred P. Sloan at the head of Amazon? Herb Kelleher of Southwest Airlines probably wouldn't have run Standard Oil as successfully as Rockefeller did. And what would a money man like ITT's Harold Geneen have done with Ben & Jerry's? It's true that many great leaders could have led other businesses to success, but it would not have been the same success those businesses found under their own leaders. And it's hard to imagine any leader in this book being capable of maximising the potential of just *any* corporation included here. You have to match the leader to the organisation.

Spot the winner

So can we use the lessons in this book to spot the winning minds of the future? It's not as obvious as you might think. Sure, some of these people – especially those who were entrepreneurs – were making money out of various enterprises even as small children. And many of those whose success was built on engineering skills were tinkering with machines before they were out of nappies. But it's refreshing to note that, just to give you a few examples:

• Robert Woodruff of Coca-Cola was a failure at school, as was Thomas Edison.
• David Ogilvy, Edwin Land of Polaroid, Ben Cohen (Ben & Jerry's), Michael Dell and many others dropped out – or were thrown out – of college.

- Many top leaders had some significant failures alongside their successes. It took Marjorie Scardino ten years to pay off her debts after the *Georgia Gazette* folded. Konosuke Matsushita started in business selling an electric light socket he'd invented – and which nobody wanted. And Bernard Marcus was fired at the age of 49 but still went on to found Home Depot.
- Several of these people didn't start to succeed in business until they were older than you might expect. For example, Sam Walton was 44 before he opened the first Wal-Mart store. Giovanni Agnelli was a 42-year-old playboy when he took over Fiat. And Ray Kroc was 54 before he discovered McDonald's and 60 before he could afford to draw an income from it.

One of the leaders in this book, David Ogilvy, said that the only way he knew to predict winners was to look at their college records (assuming they attended college). 'If they were leaders between the ages of 18 and 22' he reckoned, 'the odds are that they will emerge as leaders in middle life.' He may well be right as a rule of thumb, but you'll still find leaders who don't follow the rule. And maybe *that*'s as close as you'll get to the secret of winning leadership: great leaders – whether they are mavericks or conformists at heart – are never afraid to ignore the rules, break convention and do things their own way.

Fifty Inspirational
Business Leaders

GIOVANNI AGNELLI

1921–

Organisation: *Fiat*

Key idea: *Network*

'The heritage of my grandfather has always been to create jobs in Italy, to help the nation's balance of payments and to contribute to the Piedmontese economy.'

G iovanni Agnelli did not build up his business from scratch, but took over a thriving family firm started by his grandfather, also called Giovanni. He built up his car manufacturing empire to become Italy's largest private business enterprise, with interests in industries from oil refining to hotels, publishing to football (Fiat owns the successful Italian football team Juventus).

Agnelli positioned himself at the centre of the Italian power network, with close contacts in every significant business and political party in the country. His family became the closest thing the Italians have to a royal family, and Agnelli himself has major interests in the press, the stock exchange and in government. His influence stretched even further, with rumours of arms sales to Third World countries in contravention of international agreements, and deals with Libya's Colonel Gadafi. And all this from a man who was little more than a rich playboy until the age of 45.

Agnelli became heir to the Fiat business at the age of 14, when his father died. He enlisted with the Italian army during World War II, and switched sides when Italy surrendered in 1943, working instead for the Americans. Meanwhile Agnelli's grandfather was forced to resign, having continued to manufacture vehicles for the Axis throughout the war. He named Vittorio Valletta as his successor, although young Giovanni would own the company. At the end of 1945, Agnelli's grandfather and his mother both died within a few weeks of each other. Agnelli was 24 and head of the family and the family business.

Giovanni Agnelli ... on employee loyalty

I believe that the worker will accept the managers' authority only
if managers obtain profit through efficiency, and if efficiency, in its
turn, is obtained through a process of organisation giving new dignity
to the worker's imagination and responsibility.

Just before he died, Agnelli's grandfather gave him some advice. As
Agnelli said later, 'He told me to have a fling for a few years, to sow my
wild oats and get it out of my system, and then maybe I would become
a serious man.' On his grandfather's advice, Agnelli left Valletta to run
the business while he enjoyed himself. He was famous in the European
gossip columns for his huge casino bets, his yachts, his nightclubbing,
his passion for racing cars and, most of all, his womanising. He had a
five year on–off affair with Pamela Churchill, ex–daughter–in–law of Sir
Winston Churchill. Eventually – at Pamela's suggestion – he married
Princess Marella Caracciolo di Castagneto after she became pregnant
by him.

Agnelli continued to work at Fiat; heading up sectors of the business such as the ball-bearing enterprise. But he didn't take up the challenge of leadership until 1963 when he became managing director of
Fiat, finally assuming overall control in 1966 when he became chairman
and CEO.

Agnelli had many contacts throughout the business, finance and
political sphere in Italy, Europe and beyond. Many of these relationships had been forged or strengthened during his time as an international playboy. And now he began to build up the Fiat conglomerate
through deals struck with other influential people. Many of these deals
would be impossible in most European countries, where such influence
would not be allowed. But in Italy the system worked in Agnelli's favour,
and he knew how to get the most from it. One of his most famous connections was with Enrio Cuccia, who headed up a powerful financial
group called Mediobanca, a state-run merchant bank. Cuccia and his
allies – such as Pirelli, Olivetti and Zanussi – controlled virtually all
private industry and finance in Italy, and ensured that power remained
in the hands of the major business dynasties. Agnelli's close ties with
Mediobanca meant that no other industry stood a chance of challenging
Fiat successfully.

But Agnelli had plenty of other important contacts too. In politics,
he knew all the major figures and was regarded as an unelected poli-

Giovanni Agnelli … on leadership qualities

The manager must have understanding, flexibility and imagination. These are personal characteristics, and they are of basic importance.

tician, frequently consulted by prime ministers on key decisions, and called on to speak at political summit meetings. His contacts were both national (his sister was a minister at the foreign office, and many Italian leaders counted him among their chief advisors) and international. He spent time with the likes of Ronald Reagan and General de Gaulle, as well as being involved with the Soviets, the Libyans and other nations of dubious repute but undoubted value to Agnelli. For politicians outside Italy, Agnelli was a vital associate. Italian governments can come and go with notorious frequency but Agnelli, as Henry Kissinger once said, is 'the permanent establishment'.

Agnelli and his empire have often been criticised for their close involvement in dealings which were not necessarily squeaky clean. For ten years, the Libyan government under Colonel Gadafi owned a substantial stake in Fiat – sold to it by Agnelli in a deal which was alleged to involve the Soviets – despite the deep concerns of governments around the world. But mud has never stuck to Agnelli, who always came out of these allegations looking clean. He is seen as 'the uncrowned king', the great benefactor of the Italian people – the last person the Italians would believe ill of.

There are two reasons for this. Firstly, the Fiat conglomerate brought huge wealth and vast numbers of jobs to Italy, especially at times of economic instability. Agnelli is the richest man in Italy, controls a quarter of the Italian stock exchange, employs hundreds of thousands of people, and owns one of Italy's most popular football teams, Juventus. The second reason is that Agnelli and his family business effectively owns two of the country's leading newspapers, *La Stampa* and *Corriere della Sera*, along with several magazines, giving him significant control over the way Italian news is reported.

Agnelli stepped down as chairman and CEO of Fiat in 1996, and became honorary chairman. But he still owns the company. Under his leadership car production – Fiat's original and core business – has boomed and the rest of the empire has expanded in size, reach and control. Several highly talented managing directors have brought innovative ideas and skilful management to Fiat, contributing significantly to its success. But by far the most important factor has been Giovanni Agnelli and his influential network of contacts and associates.

WILLIAM MAXWELL AITKEN (LORD BEAVERBROOK)

1879–1964

Organisation: *Express Newspapers*

Key idea: *Never pass up a smart business merger or buy-up*

'Business is more exciting than any game.'

B
usiness, finance and politics were inextricably linked for Lord Beaverbrook, one of the leading press barons of the first half of the 20th century. Not only did he control the hugely influential Express Newspapers, he also held high government office. Inevitably, he often used his newspapers to air his political views, and to influence public opinion; this was largely the point of owning a newspaper as far as he was concerned.

Lord Beaverbrook was born Max Aitken, a Canadian from Ontario, who started out in the world of finance. After a spell selling insurance and bonds in Nova Scotia, he found he had a talent for making money. He expanded into investing and underwriting, and by 1907 he had moved to Montreal and had a seat on the Stock Exchange.

This is where he began to develop his great talent for brokering mergers and acquisitions, spotting opportunities for companies with similar business activities to amalgamate to everyone's profit, including his own. The companies he helped create in this way included The Steel Company of Canada, whose bonds found an enthusiastic market in England. Always ready to follow a keen business lead, he moved to England and settled into English life ... and English politics.

It didn't take Aitken long to get involved in politics, and by the end of 1910 he was elected an MP. Success followed him, and he soon became chief advisor to Bonar Law (a fellow Canadian), who became leader of the Conservative Party in 1911, and served briefly as Prime

Minister in the early 1920s. World War I brought more political opportunities – and disappointments. Aitken wanted to climb the ladder further, and set his sights on the Cabinet. However, his plans were thwarted when he was persuaded to give up his seat in the commons so that the person appointed to the job he had wanted (President of the Board of Trade) could be elected to the House. Never a man to give up something for nothing, Aitken's recompense for relinquishing his seat was a seat in the House of Lords instead. He was given the title Lord Beaverbrook, and soon made Minister of Information – in other words, propaganda. He had his Cabinet post.

Beaverbrook was a man of enormous energy and industry, and throughout the war he had had his finger in plenty of other pies. Two of these in particular set him up for the future. The first was his typically astute decision to buy control of a company by the name of Rolls Royce shortly after he moved to England. He made a substantial amount of money from the sale of these shares, which helped fund his later acquisitions. The second key decision – thanks to this increasing wealth – was to buy a share in the *Daily Express* in 1916. It was the newspaper that made his name.

By 1922 Beaverbrook had complete control of the *Express*. He wanted it to become one of the most influential newspapers in the country, so he invested much of his fortune in it. He had already launched the *Sunday Express* a year or so before, and now he exercised his instinct for smart business deals and bought the *Evening Standard* along with a couple of influential regional newspapers.

Beaverbrook was a dynamic and energetic leader, with an eye for popular appeal. He ran a newspaper with a high news content, a stable of regular contributors, and a varied assortment of specialist field reporters and writers from outside the staff. In his efforts to generate public loyalty to his paper, he persuaded the country's most popular cartoonist, David Low, to leave the *Star* and join the *Evening Standard*. Not only did he double Low's salary in order to win him over, he also allowed Low the unheard of permission to use his cartoons to express his own independent views. This original approach was typical of Beaverbrook's style, which was one of innovation and change, with his personality stamped all over it.

He never lost the fondness for wheeling and dealing which he learnt back in Canada, and he was constantly brokering deals and friendships, business and political mergers and takeovers. He liked to question tradition, alter patterns, disrupt continuity. In fact his friend H.G. Wells once said of Beaverbrook, 'If Max ever gets to heaven, he won't last long. He'll be chucked out for trying to pull off a merger between Heaven

William Maxwell Aitken ... on success

Three outstanding qualities make for success: judgement, industry, health. And the greatest of these is judgement.

and Hell, after having secured a controlling interest in key subsidiary companies in both places, of course.'

Beaverbrook unashamedly used his newspapers to try to influence public opinion. Often he was in the mainstream of opinion, but by no means always. On the one hand, he claimed it was his efforts that had successfully persuaded Lloyd George to resign. On the other hand, he supported appeasement towards Hitler throughout the 1930s, which turned out to be a catastrophically flawed policy. But when World War II finally broke out, it was his newspapers' finest hour.

The *Daily Express* was the most widely read newspaper in the world, and now Beaverbrook needed the outlet more than ever for his propaganda. His old friend Winston Churchill appointed him Minister of Aircraft production, a job that he took on with huge energy and enthusiasm – not to mention success. This made him one of only six members of the War Cabinet; a man Churchill wanted there for his huge drive and energy, and his reputation for getting things done regardless of any barriers of red tape that might block his way.

By the end of the 1950s, Beaverbrook had built up the circulation of the *Daily Express* to over four million. It continued to express his personal views, and he had a reputation for being tough on his editors. He freely admitted that if any of them had a differing view from his own on matters he considered important, they would be 'talked out of it'. However, the loyalty of *Express* readers owed less to their agreement with Beaverbrook's strong opinions – often on topics of little interest to them, frankly – than to his having created an original, absorbing and informative newspaper.

As he grew older, Beaverbrook renewed his interest in his native Canada, and became a generous philanthropist supporting universities and the arts. On his death, he left much of his fortune to the Beaverbrook Canadian Foundation which he created to develop projects in his homeland. He also left a thriving chain of newspapers built up almost single-handedly on the back of his immense personality and drive.

JEFF BEZOS

1964–

Organisation: *Amazon.com*

Key idea: *Obsess about customers, not competitors*

'Work hard, have fun, make history.'

J eff Bezos' story is the envy of every aspiring dotcom millionaire. He founded the first giant Internet retailer, despite overwhelming scepticism from almost everyone. First they said it couldn't work and then, when it did, they said it couldn't last. But it has lasted, and it has set the standard for every other dotcom company. And all because Jeff Bezos left a cushy job to follow an idea hardly anyone but him believed in.

Jeffrey Preston Bezos was born in Albuquerque, New Mexico. He was an extremely bright child, always fiddling with models, electronics and the like. When he was fed up sleeping in a cot, he simply found a screwdriver and took the whole thing apart. As he grew older, his family allowed him to convert the garage into his own workshop, where he indulged in such experiments as creating a solar cooker from a microwave, an umbrella and some aluminium foil.

Bezos had no trouble succeeding at school, and eventually graduated from Princeton University in 1986 with a degree in electrical engineering and computer science. He worked for a high-tech start-up organisation, and then moved to the Bankers Trust Company in New York where he developed computer systems. He was building up the skills and experience that would make him one of the most successful businessmen in the world. In 1990, Bezos moved to another Wall Street company, D E Shaw. Their interests were entrepreneurial as well as financial, and they used computers to spot market trends and to identify new business opportunities. It was only a matter of time before Bezos saw an irresistible opening.

It happened in 1994. He was looking at a Website that measured Internet usage. And he discovered that the Net was growing by 2300 per cent a year. He later described it as a wake-up call. There had to be business opportunities there, so what were they? Bezos recognised that this was the time to get online as one of the first e-commerce companies. But what should he sell?

He approached this question in typical Bezos style: methodically and analytically. He reckoned that what already sold well by mail would do well on the Net, so he researched mail-order companies. He wanted to find a product where he could create real value for customers, on the grounds that they would rather go on shopping the old way unless you could give them something online that they couldn't get any other way.

And that line of thinking led to books. A good mail-order book catalogue would be too large to be practical; the size of a telephone directory. But the Internet is designed to hold vast stores of information which can be accessed at the touch of a button. It was the obvious answer to his question. People would buy books online, if they had access to a whole library of titles they could never find in a printed catalogue.

Bezos knew very little about books, so that was his next move. Was this idea as feasible as he hoped? Incredibly, he discovered that there were just two big book wholesalers, and that books are meticulously databased. In fact, the wholesalers even had all their titles listed on CD-ROM. The product could have been designed to go online.

After analysing all the data he could get hold of, Bezos calculated that he had a 30 per cent chance of success. But he knew he'd regret it if he didn't even try. So he left his job at D E Shaw and spent the next year researching, developing and raising funds for his new business. He told all his potential investors – including his parents (who are now billionaires) – that he reckoned there was a 70 per cent chance that they would lose all their money. Nevertheless, his obvious ability and determination persuaded enough backers to get him started.

Bezos and his wife headed for Seattle to be near one of the big book wholesalers and close to plenty of Net experts. They famously started out working in their garage, using desks knocked together out of cheap doors to save money. In June 1995, Bezos and the small team he had collected around him created a hidden site and asked 300 friends to test it for them. The site was simple, fast and functional.

Amazon.com launched in July 1995. Bezos asked all 300 of his site testers to spread the word; that was all the publicity he used. In the first month, Amazon sold books in 45 countries outside the US, and every state within it. Amazon was going to succeed.

Jeff Bezos ... on attitude

Wake up every morning terrified – not of the competition but of our customers.

The business just took off and kept growing, faster than Bezos himself realised at times. On one occasion he and a colleague were sore from kneeling on the floor packing books all day. He had a brainwave, and turned to his colleague saying, 'I know what we need. Kneepads!' His co-worker calmly replied, 'What we need is packing tables.'

A year on, in May 1996, Amazon was on the front page of the *Wall Street Journal*. The publicity brought Amazon a whole new raft of customers, and finally brought the company to the attention of its huge bricks-and-mortar competitors, notably Barnes & Noble. Just as Sam Walton had done with Wal-Mart, so Jeff Bezos had crept up on the big boys and was poised to overtake them.

But Wall Street wasn't convinced. Once the likes of Barnes & Noble went online (which happened a year later), they were convinced that Amazon would be defeated for good. One analyst declared the company 'Amazon.toast'. But Amazon were way ahead of the field, and no one – not even Barnesandnoble.com – could catch them. By the end of 2000 Amazon.com was the leading online shopping site with sales of $1.92 billion, and links from over 60,000 other Websites.

Jeff Bezos is keeping one eye on his competitors. But his real focus is the customers. He firmly believes that if you look after the customers, the competition won't get a foothold. So long as Amazon has the biggest selection of books, the best prices and the easiest-to-use Website, along with the best purchase decision information, he's not going to lose sleep over Barnes & Noble or anyone else.

He likes to keep the personal touch, with his customers and his employees. For his customers, the Website allows users from around the world to read each other's reviews of products, and to buy and sell to each other through Amazon's auctions. Amazon.com is intentionally designed to be a site that feels human, not one where you feel you are interacting only with technology. Amazon employees are famously loyal, and regard their founder more as a colleague than as a boss. Many of its employees have stock options, and are already millionaires.

Jeff Bezos' vision doesn't stop here though. From the start, he was nothing if not ambitious. He doesn't just want an online bookstore, he wants an online department store. Already Amazon has expanded into

---

Jeff Bezos ... on competitive strategy on the Net

The competitive framework of the Internet changes so dynamically that if you base your strategy on what your competitors are doing, you have to change your strategy every day. If you base your strategy on what your customer actually needs, it evolves so much more slowly that you will have a more durable and robust strategy.

---

music, video, auctions and more. Bezos intends to sell everything anyone might want to buy online. That means products from clothing to cars, biscuits to garden plants. And services, too: holidays, insurance and anything else you want.

Banners the size of hoardings hang in the Amazon warehouses. They carry slogans much in the style of Wal-Mart. One banner lists the company's Six Core Values: 'Customer obsession, Ownership, Bias for action, Frugality, High hiring bar, Innovation.' (On the subject of frugality, Amazon employees still work at desks made out of doors.) Another banner spells out Jeff Bezos' vision: 'Our vision is the world's most customer-centric company. The place where people come to find and discover anything they might want to buy online.

Like many of his fellow billionaires, Bezos wants to use much of his wealth for philanthropic work. But in his natural style, he is concerned that the money should be as effective as possible. So he wants to spend time analysing the problems, calculating the likely success, and developing a long-term view. He reckons it's more effective to look a hundred years ahead than only five; the same approach he took in 1994 when he originally saw the potential for the world's first major-league online retailer.

JESSE BOOT

1850–1931

Organisation: *Boots*

Key idea: *Medicines for all*

'Cheap drugs would be dear if they were cheap and nasty. Nasty to the palate many drugs are bound to be; but worse is the nastiness of bad quality.'

J esse Boot came from a poor family, and devoted his life to improving the lot of the poor through his business. Like many successful businessmen he was a philanthropist, but in his case there was more to it than that. The whole premise of the business itself was directed at improving life for the poor.

Boot's father, John Boot, was a farm labourer, and the family lived in Hockley, an overcrowded, deprived part of Nottingham. When Jesse Boot was a young child, his father decided to open a small herbalist's shop, collecting and making his own herbal remedies together with his wife, Mary.

When Jesse Boot was ten years old, his father died. His mother continued to run the shop and, when Boot left school at thirteen, he helped his mother by collecting herbs, preparing remedies, stacking shelves, serving customers and counting up the money. In his spare time he studied pharmacy. At the age of 21 he became a partner in the business. In 1877 he took control of it, still helped by his mother.

Boot was a devout methodist, and this contributed to his deep concern about the poverty he saw around him in Nottingham, and had grown up alongside. One of the problems the poor encountered was that they frequently could not afford medicines when they were ill. The established chemists had a price-fixing policy, and doctors used to make up their own prescriptions and charge high prices for them. Boot wanted to bring basic medicines within reach of the people who needed them most.

Jesse Boot ... on making business worthwhile

If our labour is nothing to us but a means of procuring bread and butter, then our lives must be a poor thankless round of dull task work. If, however, we take up our duties in the fine healthy spirit of those who are engaged with colleagues in the common good, our business time will be bright with interest.

Boot's policy was to charge much lower prices than the other chemists and doctors for his medicines. He insisted on cash rather than credit to help keep his prices down, and he advertised extensively. He even employed a bell ringer to go round the streets of Nottingham telling people of the low prices at Boot's. This campaign was so successful that Boot doubled his takings within a month.

By 1883, Boot had moved to bigger premises and formed a private company, Boot and Company Ltd, of which he was chairman and managing director. And he began to open more stores around Nottingham. Each one was furnished in a similar style and opened to a fanfare of publicity. Many of the stores were in the poorer areas of town where property was cheaper and Boot's target customers were on the doorstep.

But the competition didn't like it. Many other chemists were hostile to Boot's low-price policy, not surprisingly, and they began to intimate that Boot's herbal products were unreliable. Luckily for Boot, the government had recently approved the right of general stores and companies to dispense medicines, taking the job out of the sole hands of doctors and chemists. So in 1894 Boot silenced his detractors by employing a qualified pharmacist and offering dispensing services. Four years later he emphasised his point again by renaming his company Boots Pure Drug Company Ltd.

By now the railway network was expanding across the country, and Boot realised that this would mean that his business could expand too. In 1884 he opened his first store outside Nottingham, in Sheffield.

By 1885 Boot was exhausted with overwork, so he took a holiday. He went to Jersey where he met Florence Rowe, the daughter of a stationer and bookseller on the island. The two soon married and Florence took an active part in the business. She introduced other products to the stores such as books, stationery and picture frames. And she started the Boots' Book Lovers Library, charging 2d to borrow a book. This brought lots of customers into the stores and, since the library counter was always at the back of the shop, they had to walk past all the other

Jesse Boot ... on his inspiration to set up in business

I had an idea that the herbalist and chemist at that time was very much out of date. Whilst other businesses were abandoning old-fashioned methods to keep pace with the progress of the age, he was merely marking time. I thought the public would welcome new chemists shops in which a greater and better variety of pharmaceutical articles could be obtained at cheaper prices.

products on their way to it. The Boots began to think of their shops as department stores rather than simply pharmacies.

The next big move came in 1891, when Boot built a new store in Pelham Street in Nottingham. It had a gallery supported by a cast iron colonnade, and the counters were made of mahogany. This was the new flagship store, and served as a model for all future Boots stores. It even had a great innovation to allow shoppers to shop on winter evenings: electric lights. The following year, Boot took over a group of properties close to the canal, the main roads and the railway station in Nottingham so that he could develop his distribution system. He employed over 80 staff here, packing and bottling, printing and advertising, and doing the accounts.

By the turn of the century Boot had 250 stores, and was acquiring other chemists' chains. Florence had the idea of opening cafés in the larger stores, which attracted still more customers, including more of the middle classes.

The Boots were very concerned for the welfare of their employees, and took good care of them. They organised frequent trips such as picnics and visits to the seaside. When Florence realised that many staff had no breakfast before they came to work, she arranged for every employee to have a cup of hot cocoa before starting work each morning. The Boots were also great benefactors, especially in their home town of Nottingham where Boot spent around £2 million on houses, parks and other amenities.

By the time of World War I, there were 560 Boots stores, with an annual turnover of £2.5 million. Boot made a big contribution to the war effort, producing water sterilisers and anti-fly cream for the front line troops. He also increased his laboratories and production capabilities to cope with demand for products which had previously been imported from Germany, such as aspirin.

By 1920 Boot was growing tired and was badly disabled by arthritis, so he sold his company for £2.25 million to a huge American pharmaceutical firm. Boot's eldest child, John, was involved with the new owners, and became chairman of Boots in 1927. Jesse Boot was granted the title Lord Trent of Nottingham in 1929, two years before his death. Another two years on, Florence opened the 1000th Boots store, and John Boot bought back the company. He continued to run it on the same principles as his father had: to serve the public and to treat the employees well.

Just like Henry Ford at around the same time, although in a completely different industry, Jesse Boot essentially made his money by recognising the value of lowering prices to attract the mass market. Coupled with a flair for marketing – more in Florence than himself – he had an unbeatable recipe. Unlike Ford, Boot also had a passionate belief in bringing his product to the masses for their benefit as well as for his own profit.

RICHARD BRANSON

1950–

Organisation: *Virgin*

Key idea: *Build a brand so distinctive it sticks to anything, and keep playing David to corporate Goliaths*

'If you can run a record company, you can run an airline. If you can run an airline, you can run a bank. If you can run a bank, you can run a soft drink company.'

R ichard Branson was born with bucketloads of entrepreneurial drive. He started his first businesses before he left school, and never looked back. And his talent for building a brand that attracts customer loyalty has enabled him to diversify into businesses as diverse as banking and soft drinks, condoms and airlines. He has an immensely clear vision of what he wants to do and how he wants to do it, and his enthusiasm spreads throughout his staff and his customers.

Branson grew up in a comfortable, middle-class Surrey home. As a child, he made his money growing Christmas trees, and left school at 16 to start a magazine, *Student*, which attracted many notable contributors, including Jean-Paul Sartre and James Baldwin. But being Branson, he couldn't sit still. So at the age of 19 he set up a mail-order record business, which evolved into a record label called Virgin Records. It was the business that launched the mega-brand.

To understand Branson's business ethos you have to recognise that he grew up in the 1960s. This was an age when the old values began to clash with the new; the hippie ideal of people before profit challenged the prevailing capitalist views. Many people of Branson's generation were proclaiming their belief in morality before money, openness rather than secrecy, innovation before convention, informality rather than formality. These were attitudes that struck a chord with Branson, and influenced his business style not only at the time but permanently.

Branson has made a career out of playing the young, idealistic David to the fat, lazy corporate Goliaths. His policy in launching new businesses is to look for a market in which the big organisations are resting complacently on their laurels; in his words, 'the big bad wolves who are dramatically overcharging and underdelivering.' Then he looks for ways to give customers far greater value.

One of his most famous companies is Virgin Atlantic, the airline he set up in the early 1980s to challenge the industry giants such as British Airways, who he felt were delivering a poor service to customers. Loving a challenge, Branson was not in the least deterred by the fact that he knew nothing about the airline business. He was a frequent flyer, and he figured he simply needed to design a service that would satisfy himself, as a typical customer.

He decided not to offer first-class accommodation at all, but to give first-class service at business-class prices. Not only did Virgin's prices undercut the competition, but its service and concern for its customers was far better. The flight crews were enthusiastic, the food was better than on other airlines, the on-board entertainment was superior. Virgin Atlantic introduced spa-style lounges in many airports; it was the first airline to offer more than two choices of meals; it was the first to install seat-back videos in every seat.

In the early 1990s, Branson sold Virgin Records for $1 billion, which put the Virgin Group on a strong financial footing. This gave Branson the means to launch businesses to challenge any Goliath he liked, even the world's most famous brand, Coca-Cola. Whilst he never expected to topple Coca-Cola from its pedestal, he managed to take a large enough share from Coca-Cola and Pepsi with his new Virgin Cola to run a very profitable business – and to strengthen his brand image as the young David (which gets harder as the business becomes ever larger itself).

Branson's skill at branding has enabled him to pull together, under the Virgin umbrella, a wide portfolio of businesses with no obvious connection other than the Virgin brand. Many of these companies have little or no relationship with each other. But Branson is clear about what makes a Virgin business, and will only put his brand on a product or service that meets his five conditions. The Virgin brand promises:

1   high quality;
2   innovation;
3   good value for money;

Richard Branson ... on creating change

There's no point in going into a business unless you shake up the whole industry. Then, you are not just making a difference for yourself. You find the whole industry has to react to your being there and change the way it does business.

4 a challenge to the traditional alternatives; and
5 a sense of fun.

The Virgin brand image is closely tied to Branson's own image, as is often the case with brands built by inspirational leaders. Branson is hugely charismatic, with a gift for publicity. He is famous for promoting Virgin businesses personally, and is always happy to appear on television, despite claiming to be deeply shy. He says he had to train himself to appear – and especially to speak – in public because he could see it was necessary for his business. According to one television producer, about 99 per cent of British chief executives turn down invitations to appear on television. But not Branson, who cannot make sense of this attitude. He argues, 'With a television spot, you are reaching ten million people. It would be bloody stupid to say no.'

Branson's publicity stunts are legendary. He launched Virgin Cola in the US by driving a tank down Fifth Avenue in New York. He is rumoured to devote a quarter of his time to public relations, and his highest paid employee is his PR and communications director. Branson reckons it's the most important job in the organisation.

His personal image supports Virgin's brand image: he dresses informally, he shows a healthy disrespect for convention, he enjoys risk-taking (such as hot air ballooning), and he appears always on the side of the customer and the ordinary person in the street. He treats his employees as colleagues rather than subordinates, giving him an informal, personal style.

And it seems to be genuine, not simply a sly PR trick. Branson disagrees with the modern tradition that the customer should always come first. He argues that employees come first, followed by customers, followed by shareholders. His logic is that well motivated and happy employees will do a better job, to the benefit of the customers. And once the customers are happy, they will keep the shareholders happy.

To this end, Branson tirelessly travels from one Virgin business to another, talking to his employees and his customers. He always carries

Richard Branson ... on using PR

Using yourself to get out and talk about your business is a lot cheaper and more effective than a lot of advertising. In fact, if you do it correctly, it can beat advertising hands down and save tens of millions of dollars.

his trademark notebook, so he can write down and action any points they raise. He encourages his staff to write to him if they have any suggestions or complaints, and his first priority each morning is to open the 25–30 letters he receives daily from his own staff. Every one is dealt with personally. Branson maintains that his staff don't need a union when they know they can come to him directly if they have a grievance.

Virgin employees get plenty of perks, including big discounts at all Virgin businesses. Branson even takes groups of employees on holiday to his private island in the Caribbean – rank and file staff who have performed well and earned the reward. As a result of all this, working for Virgin is considered an honour, and the staff are cheerful, enthusiastic and highly motivated.

Branson extends the personal touch to his customers, too. He frequently flies on Virgin Atlantic, and usually spends the flight chatting to customers, serving drinks, organising games over the tannoy system and even helping the cabin crew with their work. When the airline was smaller, Branson frequently turned up at the airport to apologise in person to passengers when a flight was late.

But beneath the friendly, affable exterior there lies, of course, an exceedingly sharp business mind. He is reputed to be ruthless and manipulative when he considers it necessary, and Tom Bower's now infamous biography of Branson suggests a less saintly personality than the public image, coupled with single-minded profiteering. Certainly, Branson knows how to cut a deal. He insists that Virgin has at least a 50 per cent stake in any company carrying its brand, and that his own managers control operations. When he set up the Virgin bank, he kept a 50 per cent stake without contributing a single penny. The money – all $500 million of it – was entirely contributed by other backers.

Branson's delight in risk taking is probably best illustrated by his taking on the British rail network. Seeing a lazy, inefficient Goliath, he decided to buy into the private system and put the Virgin brand on it. He knew that the Virgin name could be seriously tarnished by a public failure to give customers real value. He knew, too, that the train system would take years of investment before it reached the standard customers would expect – especially of a Virgin company. But Branson was keen to take the gamble, the biggest risk he'd yet taken with the Virgin name in the UK. And why? Because it was a gamble that fitted perfectly the Virgin ethos: take on the big organisations who are overcharging and underdelivering, and beat them by offering better service at better value.

ANDREW CARNEGIE

1835–1919

Organisation: *Carnegie Steel*

Key idea: *Steel*

'Put all your eggs in one basket and then watch that basket.'

C arnegie vied with his friend Rockefeller for the title of richest man in the world and, like Rockefeller, gave away the vast majority of his wealth before his death. While Rockefeller made his money from oil, Carnegie's fortune came from steel. He was one of the key players in the industrialisation of America, and he championed workers' rights.

Carnegie never forgot the poor background he had come from, and identified with his own workers as a result. He grew up in Dunfermline, in Scotland (he kept his Scottish accent all his life). He was a born salesmen, and could persuade people to do just about anything for him. As a boy he kept rabbits, and he organised his friends to go and gather food for them. In return, he named a rabbit after each of them.

Carnegie's father was a weaver, but his trade was shattered by the industrial revolution. When the steam-powered looms arrived in Scotland, thousands of hand weavers lost their jobs, including Carnegie's father. His mother earned a little opening a small shop and mending shoes and, as Carnegie wrote later, 'I began to learn what poverty meant. It was burnt into my heart then that my father had to beg for work. And then there came the resolve that I would cure that when I got to be a man.'

When Carnegie was 13, his parents decided that they must do something to avoid bringing up their family in poverty. So his mother borrowed £20 and they bought a passage to America. She already had two sisters in Pittsburgh, so that was where the Carnegies settled. Carnegie had to give up his schooling, and his father got him a job as a bobbin boy in the cotton factory where he himself had found work.

Andrew Carnegie ... on leadership

No man will make a great leader who wants to do it all himself, or to get all the credit for doing it.

Carnegie rose through a series of jobs, each one of which he did as well as he possibly could. When he worked as a messenger boy, he memorised the layout of the whole city, and the names and addresses of all the people he regularly delivered to. He also did his best to further his education, borrowing books from a local library, and staying to watch plays in the theatre when he delivered messages there in the evenings.

Eventually Carnegie joined the Pennsylvania Railroad and worked his way up to run the Pittsburgh division. He helped organise transportation during the Civil War, and saw how the iron industry grew during the war. One of Carnegie's great talents would be his ability to predict trends and to recognise potential, and he did so now. He believed the future was in iron and, with a boldness which would also become one of his trademarks, he gave up his job to start his own business.

At the time, most bridges were made of wood, and Carnegie could see that they would have to be replaced with stronger iron ones. So he started the Keystone Bridge Company. Within three years his turnover was $50,000. Carnegie was never comfortable earning money, and felt it was degrading to spend his life devoted to making as much of it as possible. Nevertheless, he seemed unable to stop. Within a few years he once again saw the future in the new refining process that enabled huge batches of iron to be converted into steel. He invested his money in the new technology, and built a new steel plant outside Pittsburgh. Employing the same technique he had done as a child with his rabbits, he named his new plant after the man he knew would be his key customer: Edgar Thomson, head of the Pennsylvania Railroad. Carnegie, always careful with money, made the most of economies of scale and was able to undercut competition.

Carnegie was one of the only industrialists of his time to support the right of workers to unionise. Although he believed what he preached, he didn't always practise it, however. One of the few blights on his career was his response to his own workers strike in 1892, calling for shorter hours and better pay. Carnegie supported his plant manager in locking out workers and hiring thugs to intimidate the workers. In the conflict, many workers were killed, and Carnegie always regretted his behaviour.

Andrew Carnegie ... on his own epitaph

Here lies a man who knew how to bring into his service men better than he was himself.

Carnegie's skills as a salesman, his boldness, and his almost un-canny ability to predict future trends meant that his business continued to expand, until by 1900 Carnegie Steel produced more steel than the whole of Britain. But J P Morgan was on his tail. He wanted to under-mine Carnegie so that his business would devalue and Morgan could buy it cheap. Carnegie fought him off successfully for a year, and was certain he could continue to do so for as long as he had to. But by 1901, Carnegie was 64, and wanted to spend more time with his family.

So he sent Morgan a note telling him how much money he wanted for Carnegie Steel. Morgan accepted almost instantly, and bought the company for just under half a billion dollars. As he concluded the deal he said, 'Congratulations, Mr Carnegie. You are now the richest man in the world.'

Carnegie had started giving away his fortune when he was still in his thirties, but once he sold his company he devoted the rest of his life to donating to good causes. He disapproved of charity, preferring to help people to help themselves, and reading and education were high on his list of ways to do this. In his book *The Gospel of Wealth*, which he wrote in 1889, he laid out his belief that all personal wealth beyond what was needed to support one's family should be treated as a trust fund to be used for the benefit of the community.

Carnegie often said that 'the man who dies rich dies disgraced.' He himself died just after the close of World War I, still worth $30 million, which he willed to various good causes. But, just like his friend John D. Rockefeller, it was only a tiny proportion of what he had already given away. During his life Carnegie had given away over $350 million.

Carnegie believed in the natural goodness of people, and was eter-nally optimistic for the future of humanity. As a result he was devas-tated by the war, which his wife later said 'broke his heart'. Carnegie had been an enthusiastic writer all his life and had kept a regular diary. But, although he survived World War I by a year, the last entry in his autobiography was the day war was declared.

STEVE CASE

1958–

Organisation: *America Online*

Key idea: *Stay in touch with the consumer*

'The competitive winners will be those with the greatest agility, the greatest ability to be flexible and opportunistic and, of course, the best ability to envision the effect on the underlying experience of consumers.'

F|or an ordinary chap, Steve Case has done pretty well for himself. In fact, one might argue that it is precisely because he's such an ordinary chap that the subscribers to America Online (AOL) feel he's on their side; an invaluable reputation to have with your customers. Unlike many successful leaders, charisma is something Case has never been credited with. But it's never held him back.

Case grew up in Hawaii where, along with his older brother, he demonstrated early entrepreneurial spirit. They ran a lemonade stand, delivered advertising circulars and had a series of other small enterprises. After Case graduated he worked in marketing related jobs for companies including Pizza Hut. He wound up as marketing manager for a very shaky business specialising in video games, called Control Video Corporation.

As the business foundered, fewer and fewer staff survived the layoffs, and Case ended up in charge of marketing with only two other key personnel left: Jim Kimsey and Marc Seriff. These three had to save the company or be out of a job. As it happened, Commodore wanted to set up an online service for Commodore 64 users (we're talking 1985 here). Control Video got involved, paying off small creditors and offering larger creditors a stake in their new company, Quantum Computer Services.

Steve Case ... on technology

Those who focus only on the fastest, most hi-tech, most powerful technologies may find that they are worshipping an idol.

As business improved, Case negotiated to provide the same service for Apple Computers and Tandy. Nevertheless, by the end of the 1980s, these three services combined had only 75,000 subscribers. So how did Steve Case build his business up to over 25 million customers by the end of 2000? As he points out himself, AOL handles 900 million emails and instant messages every day – 50 per cent more than the number of pieces of mail the US Postal Service delivers daily.

In 1989, Apple paid $2.5 million to buy itself out of the arrangement so it could launch its own service. This spurred Case and his colleagues to pull its services together under one brand. The name Case settled on was Online America (which, of course, was later swapped round to America Online).

The market may still have been small by today's standards, but it already had some big players in it. Companies such as CompuServe and Genie were offering text-based online services, and Case could see he needed to outsmart these giants if he was to find a foothold in the industry. His understanding of the consumer led him to recognise that a more user-friendly interface was the carrot which would tempt users to try his service. It worked so well that in 1991 CompuServe offered to buy out AOL for $50 million. But like other early Internet pioneers, such as Bezos and Gates, Case had faith that the industry was going to be massive. He and Kimsey turned down the offer. It was a tough decision, since they badly needed cash. So in order to raise capital they opted to go public in 1992.

AOL grew over the next few years by persistently working to create the best possible experience for the consumer. According to Case, 'Technophobes outnumber technophiles by several orders of magnitude, and it's the technophobes we need to make this new medium truly mass market. The technophiles are already aboard. Which means that "easy-to-use, fun, useful and affordable" will win every time.' In 1998 AOL turned the tables on CompuServe and acquired its online services division.

Steve Case strongly believes that most Internet users aren't interested in how the technology works; it is simply a means to an end. So he makes sure the technological developments he pursues are driven by

---

Steve Case ... on the Internet

Many businesses do not yet understand that their core franchise is dependent on the emerging interactive medium.

---

consumer need, not simply by a desire for hi-tech advances for their own sake. He aims to operate the fastest, easiest and most functional service going. And he also believes in that elusive concept, the Internet community.

Case puts great emphasis on building online communities, and being socially responsible through strategies such as integrating technology into schools, protecting consumer privacy, outlawing spamming (junk emailing) and – a practice close to the hearts of many of his customers – keeping children safe online. A parent himself, Case operates a censorship policy which aims to protect children from unsuitable material. It is a policy which some accuse of being so careful as to be overly prudish.

Case is certainly the driving force behind much of AOL's success. But one of his skills as a leader is his ability to assemble a strong team around him, each with their own complementary expertise. He has top technical and finance people, while he himself keeps a clear vision of improving the service for the regular consumer.

Steve Case is renowned for having far less ego than most of his fellow billionaires. He has famously little social personality, presence or dress sense, and can still wander the streets unrecognised – something he claims to be more than happy about. His down-to-earth attitude is much of what gives him his rapport with his customers, and has enabled AOL to make the difficult transition from being the audacious young upstart company to becoming the industry giant.

Needless to say, Case is not without his detractors. Case and his team are accused of being prudish in their censorship, of making far too many billing errors, and of giving poor technical service. Even here, however, Case's marketing flair has served him well. In 1996, when AOL had around six million subscribers, service famously went down for 19 hours. Despite initial media outrage, Case managed to spin the story into one of the enormous importance of AOL to its users. Certainly AOL has become a consumer phenomenon, and is the number one global online Internet service.

Steve Case recognises that his industry is moving at lightning speed, and that it is only a matter of time before the numerous small companies in the field consolidate into a few big ones. So he has always been ready to form mergers and make acquisitions, at a speed that often dumbfounds the experts. From AT&T to Netscape, partnerships and buyouts are critical to AOL's success, the most notable being the merger with Time Warner in 2000, giving AOL access to the content it badly needed.

Steve Case has taken his company from the small time to the big time, from Control Video Corporation to AOL-Time Warner, essentially by keeping his eye firmly on the mass-market consumer who is nervous of the Internet rather than on the handful of nerds who like flashy technology and clever gimmicks.

BEN COHEN

1951–

Organisation: *Ben & Jerry's*

Key idea: *Corporate social responsibility*

'At Ben & Jerry's, we redefined the bottom line.'

Back in the 1970s, a couple of ex-hippies unable to find decent jobs decided to start a business making ice cream... because they liked eating it. They had almost no money but hey, man, they were having fun. As it turned out they were also starting a business which would become known worldwide, and which would show other businesses a new way to have fun at work and be socially responsible too.

Ben Cohen and Jerry Greenfield both grew up on Long Island, and met in high school gym class where their shared lack of athletic talent gave them a bond that quickly turned to firm friendship. After school, Greenfield went on to a pre-med course while Cohen dropped out of college altogether. This left him unable to get a decent job. When Greenfield finished his course he applied to 20 medical schools, all of which rejected him.

The two apparent losers decided they might as well have fun, so they decided to set up in business together doing something they enjoyed. But what? Since they both loved ice cream, they enrolled on a correspondence course on ice cream making. They both passed comfortably, so it looked like an ice cream business would be easy.

They might have looked like a pair of daydreaming hippies (which they were) but they weren't stupid. They wanted to set up somewhere warm, in a rural college town where there was no competition. They couldn't find a suitable location, however, so they decided that lack of competition was the most important criteria and they settled on a town in Vermont called Burlington.

Ben & Jerry's started out in 1978 in a run-down ex-petrol station with only a few thousand dollars between them. However, as well as running an ice cream parlour, they decided to sell their ice creams to other stores. Cohen was the salesman of the pair, and he persuaded stores to take the ice cream on sale or return. He knew that despite their lack of experience, assets or money, the one thing they did have was damn good ice cream. He was right. From the start, Ben & Jerry's ice cream was famously rich, high-fat and creamy, and the flavours had bizarre names such as Cherry Garcia, Chunky Monkey and Phish Food. The stuff sold, and Cohen and Greenfield were in business. Soon, they were distributing their ice cream all over New England.

And then something extraordinary happened – extraordinarily lucky, although it didn't seem it at the time. The luxury ice cream manufacturer Häagen-Dazs had just been bought by a company called Pillsbury, a corporation whose symbol was a white mascot known as the doughboy. Pillsbury must have realised how good Ben & Jerry's ice cream was, because they told all their customers that they wouldn't allow them to stock Häagen-Dazs if they also sold Ben & Jerry's.

Cohen and Greenfield were in danger of seeing their business go down the chute, and all their hippie hackles were raised by this big corporation threatening them (and, in effect, their suppliers too). So they sued. Not only did they sue, but they also launched a big campaign against Pillsbury's tactics, using the slogan 'What's the doughboy afraid of?' Suddenly, this small company had national exposure and sympathy. The media attention put so much pressure on Pillsbury that they eventually capitulated. By now, Ben & Jerry's ice cream was so well known, it was being sold in stores and through franchises right across the country. It has kept expanding ever since, going public in 1984.

But Cohen and Greenfield weren't as happy as you might think. As the business grew, they felt they were turning into exactly the kind of stereotypical businessmen they had always despised. They were so despondent about this departure from their true ideals that they nearly sold the company. Cohen was complaining about this predicament one day to a friend of his who said, 'If you don't like the way business is done, why don't you change it?'

So that's what they did. Cohen and Greenfield looked for ways to make their company more socially responsible. And they came up with a new approach that suited their principles – still founded on the ideals of the 1960s – and made for good business too.

To begin with, Ben & Jerry's had always looked after its employees. And as it grew, it found new ways to do this. It set up an evaluation system by which employees were asked to give an annual evaluation of their

Ben Cohen ... on realism

Expecting people to accomplish things that they're not able to do is bad for business, because it creates an atmosphere of failure, criticism, and never being good enough.

supervisor, and gave them proper training in how and why they were doing this. They included employees in developing benefits packages; when a group of employees commented on the lack of day-care facilities and asked the company to help, management's response was to set up a worker committee to decide how to set up and run a day-care scheme.

Cohen and Greenfield created teams of workers to design their own work procedures, and to advise on the design of their new manufacturing and distribution plants. Job applicants had to be interviewed by the team of employees as well as the supervisor, so they would feel involved, and have a stake in the new person's success. And employees were offered a portfolio of benefits from which they could choose, instead of a fixed package. So someone could opt out of the healthcare programme and use the saving to increase their childcare allowance, for example. For a long time, Ben & Jerry's had a policy limiting the salary of the highest-paid manager to no more than seven times the total salary (including benefits) of the lowest-paid employee. (They eventually had to abandon this when they brought in an outside CEO.)

Cohen and Greenfield had developed employee relations even the most dyed-in-the-wool hippie could be proud of. And they wanted to do the same with their social policies. They believed in supporting the local community, so they used only milk and cream from family run farms in Vermont, the company's home state – a policy which they still manage to apply. Since they also wanted to help disadvantaged communities, they source suppliers in suitable areas. All the brownies in Ben & Jerry's Chocolate Fudge Brownie ice cream comes from a New York inner city bakery.

Cohen and Greenfield also started the Ben & Jerry's Foundation, through which the business donates 7.5 per cent of its pre-tax profits to good causes. That's around four times the average level of corporate giving. Ben & Jerry's contributes to the community in numerous ways, usually with the emphasis on helping people to help themselves. For example, the company will sometimes 'donate' a store to a not-for-profit organisation in a disadvantaged area by waiving the franchise fees. Profits go to helping local community action agencies. Employees

Ben Cohen ... on entrepreneurial roles

We started off as the people who gave birth to and nurtured an idea. Then we became the supervisors of a crew of people who were carrying out our ideas. Then we became the co-captains leading a team of people committed to a common goal. Then we became the coaches sitting on the sidelines trying to help the team on the field, coupled with being the team mascots.

sometimes even take cuts in pay to work at these stores because it gives them a job they can really believe in.

By the early 1990s Greenfield had pulled back from active management, and in 1995 Cohen decided to step down as CEO, although he stayed actively involved as chairman. The new CEO oversaw the businesses expansion into new markets – especially in Europe – and new products such as sorbets and frozen yoghurts. Cohen maintained his principles, arguing against selling into France as a protest against its nuclear testing policies, and against making sorbets because it didn't help the Vermont dairy industry. But he had learned realism as well as idealism, and he allowed the majority view on the board to prevail.

Ben & Jerry's crazy hippie ideas weren't so crazy after all. The company is now the most profitable ice cream producer in the world, largely because of its high levels of employee involvement and loyalty, and its sympathetic image as a socially responsible business. In April 2000, Ben & Jerry's was bought by Unilever for about $326 million, in a deal which Cohen had made sure would preserve its integrity, and help expand its principles into Unilever as well.

Ben & Jerry's would remain a separate though wholly owned subsidiary, with both Cohen and Greenfield on the board. Unilever agreed to continue to put 7.5 per cent of Ben & Jerry's pre-tax profits into a foundation, and to preserve jobs and continue to make the ice cream in the same way. Unilever also agreed to contribute $5 million to the foundation, to distribute $5 million to employees, and to create another $5 million fund to help organisations in poor neighbourhoods.

In the statement Cohen released when the deal was announced, he quoted the lyrics of a song by the Grateful Dead: 'Once in a while you get shown the light in the strangest of places if you look at it right.' A multi-billion-dollar corporation was certainly the strangest of places for an anti-establishment maverick like Cohen to find the light. But then, perhaps, it was he who showed *them* the light ...

MICHAEL DELL

1965–

Organisation: *Dell Computer Corporation*

Key idea: *Mass customisation*

'The total customer experience – including an emphasis on service and speed – is the next competitive frontier.'

I f you can spot a future millionaire while they are still at school, you could have predicted Michael Dell would have done well for himself. Like many great business leaders, he couldn't wait until he had grown up to get started. His first few businesses are reminiscent of many of the other winning minds who have made it into this book.

At 12, Dell earned $2000 from a mail-order business trading stamps. By 16, he was selling subscriptions to the Houston Post making himself $18,000 in a year in commission. His economics teacher at school knew nothing of this until she set the class the assignment of filling out their own tax returns. She thought Dell had put the decimal point in the wrong place. She was mortified when she discovered that he hadn't, and was actually earning more than she was.

But Dell's real fascination – alongside making money – was computers. In 1980, at the age of 15, he bought an Apple II computer. The first thing he did with it was take it to pieces to find out how it worked. His ability to put it back together again at all probably sets him apart from most of us, but he did rather better than that. He saw a way to make a fortune out of assembling computers.

The next step on Dell's road to fortune was an unofficial business selling upgraded PCs from his room at college. At the end of his first year his business was seriously interfering with his education. His parents – understandably sceptical of his desire to set up in competition with IBM

– urged him to abandon his computer business, but in the end he opted to quit college instead and register his company.

Dell Computers was founded in 1984, on the back of Dell's revolutionary idea that you could sell computers direct to customers. The universal practice at the time was to buy your computer from a retailer who, in turn, bought it from a manufacturer and stuck on a 50 per cent mark-up. Dell started by selling upgraded PCs, but soon realised that he could make his own from scratch by buying in and assembling the component parts. What's more, each customer could order any permutation they wanted and you could assemble the computer to order. It was this idea of mass customisation that formed the foundation of a billion pound business.

As so often happens, the competition – which was led by Compaq and IBM – wrote off this new company. But Dell's idea gave him competitive advantage in several ways. For a start, his computers were cheaper than anyone else's because he had cut out the middleman. And he could deliver fast to customers. But he could also customise computers by assembling any feasible combination of components for his customers. What's more, he was able to shave his costs down with highly flexible inventory management. Dell had learnt this particular lesson the hard way, in 1989, when he bought in more chips than he needed and then got caught as prices slumped; the technology advanced and no one wanted the obsolete chips at all.

So Dell's policy is to set up close relationships with suppliers and carry minimal stock. The company only carries about seven days inventory (compared with two to three months for its competitors), and is working constantly to reduce this even further. It can only be done through what Michael Dell terms 'virtual integration': relationships between manufacturer, supplier and customer which are almost seamless.

This kind of inventory management has another huge advantage, too, in a fast moving, high-tech industry such as Dell's. While everyone else is fretting about forecasting consumer trends, it barely makes any difference to Dell. They can respond so fast they don't need advance warning. As Dell says, 'If I've got 11 days of inventory and my competitor has 80, and Intel comes out with a new 450-megahertz chip, that means I'm going to get to market 69 days sooner.'

Dell's early business ventures when he was still at college were about customising computers, and he has always had his eye firmly fixed on what the customer wants. He recognises the need to build customer loyalty, and believes that the best way to do it is by listening to customers. He aims to give excellent customer service, and authorises his em-

Michael Dell ... on virtual integration

There is an inverse correlation between the amount of information you have and how many assets you need.

ployees to bend the occasional rule for customers who have a special case. As far as e-shopping is concerned, Dell believes that the shopping experience is a greater driver of customer loyalty than traditional factors such as price or product.

And he should know. Dell intends to move his entire business on-line eventually, and has led the way in selling computers on the Internet. www.dell.com was launched in 1996, and now reports online sales of $50 million a day – the largest online commercial seller of computer systems. Not only do Dell offer online purchasing, however, but a huge proportion of its technical support and order-status transactions now happen online.

Another area of tight competition in the IT sector is recruitment. It is increasingly difficult to attract the best people, and Michael Dell has successfully applied his brand of leadership to this problem, too. He operates a policy of succession planning; in other words, it is each manager's responsibility to recruit their own successor. This helps to ensure a high quality workforce of motivated people. If Dell Computers identify a talented person for whom they have no vacancy, they will create a post simply to get them on board.

As the business expands, many employees find their workload increases too. So Dell has a policy of splitting jobs when an employee is becoming overworked. To begin with, many people felt threatened when half their job was taken away. But the system is now commonplace and employees have learnt that their responsibilities – and their new workload – soon grow to the point where they may well need to split again. In fact, Dell has even split his own job more than once.

Dell offers his employees a good working environment with career opportunities, thorough training, and incentives such as profit-sharing and stock options. He knows this works because he has researched what it is that encourages people to stay at Dell. And certainly he has a high staff retention rate.

There is a conventional wisdom that states that entrepreneurs who are good at starting up companies are rarely talented at managing them once they become large organisations. Michael Dell bucks this trend, and is repeatedly singled out as businessman of the year, CEO of the

---

Michael Dell ... on satisfying customers

The total customer experience – including an emphasis on service and speed – is the next competitive frontier.

---

year and the like, in publications from *PC Magazine* to *Business Week*. Managing growth has been an enormous challenge for Dell, whose business grew from almost nothing in 1984 to well over 20,000 employees by the end of the 1990s ... and is still growing.

One of Dell's key strategies for coping with growth is to segment the business whenever it reaches a critical size. This way he is never running any business too large or inflexible. He simply splits it into manageable segments along market lines, so each group of customers has its own segment. It is designed as a recipe to accommodate massive levels of growth. At his present rate, he's going to need it.

WALT DISNEY

1901–1966

Organisation: *Disney Corporation*

Key idea: *Trust the public, not the critics*

'If you can dream it, you can do it.'

Walt Disney created the first ever multimedia corporation, he invented the theme park, and he came up with the first ever full-length animated movie. What's more, he gave us Mickey Mouse. The image Disney cultivated and promulgated throughout his life was that of a happy, avuncular soul who wanted nothing more than to bring entertainment to children and adults around the world. But Disney's public image was nowhere near the truth. He possessed no avuncular spirit whatever, but was a dark and controlling personality. However, he also had extraordinary vision and the talent to realise it.

Disney had a pretty miserable childhood, born into poverty in Chicago with a father who gave him no affection but plenty of beatings. One of Disney's favourite places of escape from his father was in art classes, where he found his skill in drawing. His first job was as a commercial artist, where he began to get into the new field of animation. It appealed to Disney because it had a strong technical content, and because it fulfilled his need for escapism: a cartoon was a chance to complete a whole self-contained world.

Disney served his share of lean times, earning a pittance and barely able to afford to feed himself. But before long he moved to Los Angeles and teamed up with his brother Roy, who looked after the business side of things for Walt. Success arrived when Disney created Mickey Mouse, a character perfectly in tune with the times. America was going through the Depression, and Mickey was cheery, mischievous and endlessly

Walt Disney ... on team building

Of all the things I've done, the most vital is co-ordinating the talents of those who work for us and pointing them towards a certain goal.

inventive – a symbol of the irrepresible spirit of America even when times were hard.

But not only did Disney recognise the spirit of the times in Mickey's personality, he also had the technical ingenuity to add to his appeal. Disney was the first animator to add music and sound effects to a cartoon, making Mickey Mouse even more popular than he would otherwise have been.

Much of Disney's strength lay in this talent for developing and incorporating new technology and new ideas to draw audiences. He was eager to use Technicolor, he produced the first ever full-length animated feature – *Snow White and the Seven Dwarfs* – and he was the first Hollywood boss to see the potential of television.

By the 1930s Disney's team of artists began to expand and the Corporation grew. By 1940 the Corporation employed 1000 people: animators, technicians, artists and story men. The Disney brand represented escapist, popular, safe films that you could confidently take your children to. To the critics his productions were often naïve, sentimental and even banal, but he didn't care. They drew the crowds. As Disney said, 'We are not trying to entertain the critics. I'll take my chances with the public.'

In fact, although Disney never tackled tough, controversial or even merely uncomfortable subjects, he wasn't the conservative he might have appeared. On a personal level he was withdrawn, and he clearly felt deeply uneasy with material that uncovered any emotion that was more than superficial. But he was a radical when it came to technology. He was far less interested in content than in developing new technologies from colour and sound in the early days through to his ultimate achievement: Disneyland.

By the 1950s and 1960s, Disneyland was occupying most of Disney's attention. He was a gambler when he really believed in the commercial possibilities of an idea; he had risked everything on *Snow White and the Seven Dwarves*, while his critics insisted that no one would watch an animated cartoon that ran for 90 minutes. Now Disney gambled his whole business on the success of Disneyland – he even mortgaged his

Walt Disney ... on competition

I have been up against tough competition all my life. I wouldn't know how to get along without it.

personal insurance to raise the $17 million he needed to launch his big idea.

Disney believed – in spite of the many critics who predicted financial disaster – that people would flock to a place where anything unpleasant, distasteful or mundane was eliminated in favour of excitement, fantasy and dreams. Even the scariest features were safe and unthreatening. Disney put huge energy into planning Disneyland, which excited him far more than the movies. Here was real 3-D, walk-in escapism. It incorporated urban planning features and visionary design to prove Disney right and confound his critics. By 1980, Disneyland had welcomed over 200 million visitors through its gates. Disney World in Florida was Disney's next great project, begun in the early 1960s and finally opened, after Disney's death, in 1971.

Walt Disney was a smarter businessman than he often appeared to his critics. He understood earlier than many people the value of branding, and protected the Disney brand fiercely. He kept firm control over his organisation, ensuring that every Disney production fitted the Disney image. He understood what the great American (and eventually global) public wanted, and ignored charges of sentimentality and anodyne storylines, concentrating on what the public clearly wanted, and voted for with their feet. In other words, he was truly customer focused.

At the same time, Disney had a clear vision of where he wanted to be, and made sure he embraced new technology as a means of striding towards his goal ahead of the competition. He is an American hero, worshipped by many including Amazon.com's founder, Jeff Bezos, who sees Disney as a role model. In his words, 'The thing that always amazed me was how powerful his vision was. He knew exactly what he wanted to build and teamed with a bunch of really smart people and built it. Everyone thought it wouldn't work ... But he did it.'

THOMAS EDISON

1847–1931

Organisation: *Thomas A Edison Inc.*

Key idea: *The electric light bulb*

'Genius is one percent inspiration, ninety-nine percent perspiration.'

E dison has been called the most influential figure of the millennium. Famous for the invention of electric light and the phonograph, he actually obtained 1093 patents during his life, more than twice as many as anyone else in history. He worked on the principal that he would only develop commercial ideas, with the result that he built up a hugely profitable organisation. And all this from a man who was ninety per cent deaf and had no formal education.

Edison was born, the youngest of seven children, in Milan, Ohio. He didn't do particularly well at school, and was accused of asking too many questions and having a poor attention span. When one of the teachers described his mind as 'addled' his mother lost her patience with the school and removed her son. From then on she taught him at home. After a while a tutor had to be brought in to teach him science, since his parents could no longer answer any of his questions on the subject.

By the time he was 12, Edison's family had moved to Port Huron, Michigan, and he started working on the railroad selling newspapers and snacks. He also ran a couple of other small enterprises on the side. After a while, he discovered that details of the debate between Lincoln and Douglas were being teletyped into the station each day. He promptly set up his own newspaper – the *Weekly Herald* – to broadcast this information, operating out of a station carriage. It was the first newspaper ever to be typeset, printed and sold on a train.

By the age of 13 he was earning enough money to pay his own keep, and had change over to set up a chemical laboratory to test all the experiments he read about. Unfortunately, he stored some of the chemicals in a train cupboard and one day, after spilling some of them, he accidentally set fire to the baggage car. It was the end of his on-board career, and he could only sell his papers at stations after that.

One day, while hanging around the station as usual, Edison saw the station master's three-year-old son wander onto the track as a train was approaching. He moved fast to save the child, and the station master rewarded him by teaching him how to use the telegraphy machine, a skill he would later find extremely useful.

Edison had not been born deaf but round about this time he began to lose his hearing, possibly as a result of scarlet fever. Before long he was totally deaf in one ear, and eighty per cent deaf in the other. As he grew used to it, he rather liked the ability the silence gave him to concentrate. In later life he was offered an operation that would restore some of his hearing but turned it down. He was afraid he would have to relearn how to think in an atmosphere where noise could distract him.

At 14, Edison began working as a telegraph operator, and soon began travelling round the US doing telegraph work. In 1868, at the age of 21, he took a job in Boston where he could work out of business hours on his experiments. In less than a year he had given up work so he could pursue his inventing full time. The first invention to receive a patent was an electric vote recorder. However, the politicians were reluctant to buy it since a faster process in the Legislature would deny them valuable time to change their colleagues' opinions during the vote counting. Edison was discouraged by his failure to sell his new invention, and determined never again to waste time inventing things nobody wanted.

Edison next moved to New York, pennilesss by now, where a friend let him sleep in a room at the financial company where he worked. In typical style, Edison used to wander around the offices after hours studying the machinery and equipment and learning how it worked. One day he happened to be in the building when one of the stock-ticker machines broke down. The office manager was panicking because no one gathered around the machine knew how to repair it. Edison managed to elbow his way to the front and offered to try to fix it. Within moments, he had it working perfectly again. The manager was so grateful, he instantly hired Edison on double the average electrician's salary, as a maintenance engineer.

Edison continued inventing, and started to receive several patents for improvements to the telegraph. Before long, a corporation paid him the first money he had ever received for any of his inventions – $40,000 for some patent rights. He had never seen money like it. He set up an electrical engineering firm and began inventing full time. A few years later he sold the firm and used the proceeds to set up his own laboratory in Newark, New Jersey in 1873, at the age of 26.

Thomas Edison … on failure

I have not failed. I've just found 10,000 ways that don't work.

Edison was inventing improvements to telegraphy constantly, and also working on the phonograph. At the same time, Alexander Graham Bell was working on the invention of the telephone. (Curiously, Bell almost invented the phonograph first, and Edison the telephone.) Edison moved his laboratory again, this time to Menlo Park, New Jersey, and in 1877 he finally invented the first phonograph (which remained his favourite invention). He also patented the carbon transmitter, which made Bell's telephone audible enough to use.

Edison was frustrated that Bell was ahead of him in his invention of the telephone, but he managed to steal his thunder, so to speak, by coming up with an even more impressive invention of his own: the first commercially practical electric light bulb. Not only that, but he followed it by inventing the power station – a central generating and distribution system for supplying electricity to an entire city. Edison formed several companies to manufacture and supply the apparatus needed for the new system, and took his invention abroad and set up companies overseas as well.

By 1892, the Edison General Electric Co. merged with Thomson-Houston to form the General Electric Corporation, in which Edison had a major stake. Edison continued to generate inventions and set up companies to market them. He developed the first disc phonograph (the earlier model having used wax cylinders), the first silent film (in 1904), and the first 'talking' picture (in 1911).

In 1911, Edison merged all his companies into Thomas A Edison Inc. This large organisation required dedicated management, and Edison removed himself from much of the day-to-day running. The company's priority was to maintain and increase sales rather than produce new inventions. Edison continued work in his laboratory and, in later years, in his lab at home. During World War I, Edison was made head of the Naval Consulting Board, and did a lot of work on submarine detection. He said later that he was 'proud of the fact that I never invented weapons to kill.'

Edison was the most extraordinarily prolific inventor, and an exceptionally hard worker, who at times neglected his family in favour of work. He was shy and quite a cold man, often impatient and with relatively few friends. Work was his life. He claimed that 'The three things

Thomas Edison ... on thinking

Thinking is hard work ... From his neck down a man is worth a couple of dollars a day. From the neck up he is worth anything that his brain can produce.

that are essential to achievement are hard work, stick-to-it-iv-ness, and common sense.' He had thousands of failures as well as successes – many of the failures led to later successes – and the quantity of his output was probably his most notable characteristic.

Edison was also happy to share the workload, and worked alongside many noted scientists and many on his own staff. Although he invented the phonograph in 1877, it was his chief machinist who actually constructed the prototype. Edison's lack of formal scientific training – coupled with his determination to be commercial – may explain why he is credited with only one true scientific discovery: the Edison Effect, concerning the flow of electrons from a heated filament. Many of his inventions were improvements or adaptations to existing inventions, often his own.

Edison received his final patent at the age of 82, after which his health began to fail. Two years later, on 18 October 1931, he died. That evening, countless people and corporations around the world paid their respects by dimming their electric lights in his memory.

ENZO FERRARI
1898–1988
Organisation: *Ferrari*

Key idea: *Racing cars get priority*

'I build engines and attach wheels to them.'

T he name Ferrari, more than that of any other car, summons up the idea of speed. Ferrari cars have the archetypical style and elegance of almost all Italian cars and motorbikes, but their true purpose is simply to go faster than any other car. That's because Enzo Ferrari, their founder, was a racing driver turned manufacturer, who only started making sports cars to bolster up the finances of his racing car business.

Ferrari grew up in Modena in northern Italy, where his father ran a metal fabrication business. At the age of 10, Ferrari's father took him to his first motor race in Bologna. Ferrari began going to races whenever he could, and decided he wanted to become a racing car driver himself. By the time he was 13 he had learnt to drive. In 1916, the year he left school, Ferrari was shattered by the death of both his father and his brother. He served in the war and then, in 1918, was almost killed by the flu epidemic.

On his recovery, Ferrari was still determined to pursue his dream of racing cars. But he needed work, too. He applied for a job at Fiat but was turned down, so he ended up working as a delivery driver for a local carmaker, and test driving in between deliveries. He took up racing more seriously and started to have the occasional success. As a result, a friend of his managed to get him a job with Alfa Romeo as a test driver, a position that led to Ferrari becoming a racing driver for Alfa Romeo. Ferrari worked his way up to racing in more important races, until eventually he was given the task of racing for Alfa Romeo in the French Grand Prix, the most prestigious race of the year.

He flunked it. It seems that Ferrari lost his confidence in his own racing ability, and couldn't take part in the race. In fact, he was probably right. Although he was a talented racing driver, he was never likely to become a world champion. After a couple of years, he returned to a successful career racing in minor events.

It was while Ferrari was racing for Alfa Romeo that he encountered the father of the famous World War I ace Francesco Baracca, who was so impressed by Ferrari that he suggested Ferrari use his son's squadron badge. It depicted a prancing horse, the symbol Ferrari later chose for his own cars' insignia. (He added a yellow background because it is the colour of Modena.)

Ferrari continued to work for Alfa Romeo as a driver and as a salesman, but in 1929 he decided to start his own company, the Scuderia Ferrari, a novel business idea. This company organised racing for the wealthy clients – including Alfa Romeo – who were its members: the Scuderia delivered the car to the race, and provided mechanical support and any other services required. The cars were all Alfa Romeos, so Ferrari got Alfa Romeo to guarantee technical assistance with the cars in exchange for stock in Ferrari's company. He made similar arrangements with Pirelli, Shell and Bosch.

But it was the drivers Ferrari managed to sign to his team who were the greatest ingredient in his success. In the Scuderia's first year Ferrari had 50 drivers, some full time, including many big names in the racing world. None was paid a salary, but they received a share of the prize money. They competed in 22 events and won eight, with many good placings in others. The team was the largest ever put together by an individual, and it was a sensation.

But in 1933, trouble hit. Alfa Romeo announced it was withdrawing from racing due to financial problems. This meant that Ferrari's supply of cars would dry up. However Ferrari, with the help of Pirelli, persuaded Alfa Romeo to take a different course. They would provide Ferrari with six racing cars, and the services of its engineer and test driver. The Scuderia would become the racing department of Alfa Romeo.

It was at about this time that Ferrari gave up racing himself, when his eldest son was born. But by now, his ambitions had extended much further, and he could see the potential for business success, which appealed to him even more. Many of his contemporaries noted that Ferrari, especially later in his life, was a businessman first and a racing enthusiast second, despite his undoubted passion for racing.

In 1937, Alfa dealt Ferrari another blow. They decided to bring their racing operations back in house. This meant that Ferrari, instead of being in charge of his own business, was being brought under the Alfa

Enzo Ferrari ... on car design

Aerodynamics are for people who cannot build engines.

umbrella, and expected to work as Direttore Sportivo under someone else. He couldn't do it.

Ferrari soon left, under an agreement that banned him from setting up in competition with Alfa for four years. Unable to build racing cars, he produced car parts for various clients for the next few years.

After the interruption of World War II, Ferrari finally decided to create his own Grand Prix car. He was nearly 50, and the height of his career had been a long time coming. In 1947 Ferrari's first Grand Prix car was unveiled, and by the early 1950s, Ferrari was dominating the racing world.

Building world-class racing cars – and then racing them – is an expensive business, and Ferrari needed more income. So he began to build road cars as a way to subsidise his racing programme, as he put it. This was, of course, the opposite direction from that in which other car manufacturers were generally working. But Ferrari wasn't just racing for fun. He wanted to be a big name in business too. And his sports cars certainly became famous, for their innovative design and powerful engines.

Ferrari was still a relatively small company, though, and Enzo Ferrari was having trouble meeting the demand for their sports cars and maintaining his racing programme. Ford tried to buy the company in 1963, but Ferrari wouldn't sign unless Ford agreed to let him run the racing side of the business. Ford refused. Finally, in 1969, Gianni Agnelli came to his rescue and Fiat bought a 50 per cent share in Ferrari. Ferrari was still in charge, but he had the backing of the Fiat empire. By now, Enzo Ferrari was held in awe and admiration by most of Italy, and Agnelli was no exception.

One of Ferrari's skills as a leader was his lack of sentimentalism about his business. He could see that he needed more financial muscle, so he sold half his company without regret, and in a deal that left Fiat a further 40 per cent on his death. It had been a trademark of his all along. Whenever he produced a car that didn't succeed, or didn't sell, he simply destroyed it; broke it up for scrap and reused what he could. Consequently almost no early Ferraris still exist. Ferrari ruled with a strong hand, although he was a genial man, and he became a legend throughout his home country and across the racing world.

Enzo Ferrari ... on leaders

A company is perfect when the number of partners is uneven and less than three.

Eventually, Ferrari lost its top place in the racing world to the big German companies Mercedes and Auto Union. They put their efforts into aerodynamics and bodywork while Ferrari was still preoccupied with engines and mechanics. But it never fell out of the running altogether, and in the mid-1970s Ferrari was still winning titles with his beloved Formula 1 cars with Niki Lauda at the wheel.

Enzo Ferrari died in 1988 at the age of 90, a legend in Italy for his creation of one the country's most famous products. He led his company with the same courage and single-mindedness with which he raced cars, and the result is that, years after his death, the Ferrari brand is as strong as ever, and the Ferrari Formula 1 team is back in the world championship stakes.

HENRY FORD

1863–1947

Organisation: *Ford Motors*

Key idea: *Mass production*

'If we have a tradition it is this: everything can always be done better than it is being done.'

enry Ford is believed by many to be the greatest businessman of the 20th century. He invented mass production, and has been credited with creating the American middle class. He built a business in one of the toughest markets going – the auto business in early 1900s America was a hugely oversubscribed new industry. Towards the end of his life he blotted his copybook seriously, but it is a mark of the respect the business world holds him in that even with a damaging black mark on his reputation, he still ranks as one of the world's greatest.

Henry Ford was the eldest of six children and grew up on his family's farm. He studied in a one-room school and did chores around the farm. Life was comfortable but not luxurious – his relatively modest roots were to influence some of his key decisions in the future. Ford didn't much care for helping around the farm, but was always happier tinkering with machinery. Leaving school at 16, he went to work in various machine shops around Detroit. He operated and repaired steam engines, and continued to help around the farm, especially fixing farm machinery.

By 1896 he was chief engineer at the Detroit Edison electric plant, spending his spare time building a horseless carriage in his backyard shed. He called it the quadricycle – it had four wheels and was steered with a tiller – and when it was completed he couldn't fit it through the door, so he had to knock down part of the wall before he could drive it out.

Ford took his quadricycle around to potential investors, and managed to find backing for it. So in 1903, he formed the Ford Motor company, where two or three men produced a few cars a day, building them from components made to order by other companies. By 1905, the fledgling automobile industry was starting to take off, with around fifty new companies a year trying to get in on the scene. Ford's backers told him the way to make money was to build a car for wealthy people to compete with Cadillac and the like. But Ford disagreed.

Ford didn't come from a wealthy background, and he thought people like him should be able to buy cars. He reckoned the men who built the cars should be able to own them. After strong disagreements with his backers, he finally bought them out, and designed a car that was simple, functional and relatively inexpensive: the Model T. It was launched in 1908, cost $850 and, as Ford famously proclaimed, 'You can have any colour you want, so long as it's black.'

The Ford Model T was the most successful vehicle ever made in the US. It survived for nearly twenty years, during which time over 15.5 million were built. It was a simple car to drive, easy to maintain and it even drove well on uneven roads. Ordinary people could afford to buy the Model T – a new car-owning middle class began to emerge – and the horse disappeared so fast from American roads that Ford is sometimes credited with initiating an agricultural revolution as farmers cut right back on hay production and turned over to other crops.

In yet another of Ford's many insights, he realised that people wanted to buy their cars locally, not from some distant manufacturer based halfway across the country. So he invented the dealer-franchise system to make and service his cars. By 1912 Ford had licensed 7000 of these local Ford dealers across the US. Ford also used his powerful position to push for gas stations across the country, and then for better roads for his customers to drive their cars on; his campaign finally resulted in the interstate highway system of which America is still so proud.

By 1918, half of all the cars on American roads were Model Ts, and Ford had had to find new ways to supply the mass demand he had created. Initially, his cars were mounted on cradles and pushed around from one group of workers to the next. But this wasn't fast enough. So in 1913 Ford restructured the whole production system. As he put it, 'The man who puts in a bolt does not put on the nut; the man who puts on the nut does not tighten it …'. Part-built cars were roped together so they could be pulled at a steady speed past the workers. Ford had invented the moving assembly line. In one year, production increased by almost double to 200,000, and the number of workers dropped by 1500

Henry Ford ... on time management

Time waste differs from material waste in that there can be no salvage.

---

to 12,880. In 1914, the first automatic conveyor belt could produce a car every 93 minutes.

But the number of workers was posing a problem for Ford. The work was so mind-numbing that only ten per cent of the workers he hired actually stayed. In order to resolve this, he came up with an ingenious solution: he raised wages from $2.30 a day – standard in the industry – to $5 a day. It worked. Workers came from all over the country to his factory, and his assembly line technique meant that unskilled men such as ex-farm workers could easily do the job. Ford was concerned that they would fritter away their new wealth on alcohol and tobacco (which Ford believed was bad for the health), so he formed the Sociological Department to visit workers in their homes and hand out leaflets advising them on how to live cleanly and healthily. There was one thing, however to which Ford was opposed: unionisation. (Eventually, in the 1930s, he became the last car manufacturer to unionise his workforce.)

This new, well-paid breed of worker became the backbone of the new middle class – the comfortably-off blue-collar worker. They could afford to run a home and support a family and – as Ford had planned – to buy a car. During Ford's childhood, 75 per cent of Americans lived in rural areas. But things were changing, and Ford was hastening that change. People moved to the cities to work in the factories, and once they could afford cars they could live wherever they liked.

Ford's company now began to build the largest industrial complex in the world beside the Rouge River in Dearborn, Michigan, Ford's home town. Ford had come up with yet another revolutionary idea: vertical integration. The Rouge Plant incorporated everything Ford needed for his 100,000 workers to make cars: a glass factory, a steel mill, rolling mills and forges to make springs and car bodies, cylinder heads and wheels. Iron ore and coal were brought in via the Great Lakes and along the railroads. Ford controlled Brazilian rubber plantations, iron-ore mines, thousands of acres of timber, a fleet of ships ... Ford Motor's car production was self-sufficient.

Ford, however, despite being a genius of a management thinker, was no manager. He spent far too little time running the business and spent more time on the factory floor, and involved in other pursuits such

---

Henry Ford ... on self-belief

One of the great discoveries man makes, one of his great surprises, is to find he can do what he was afraid he couldn't do. Most of the bars we beat against are in ourselves – we put them there, and we can take them down.

---

as standing (unsuccessfully) for senate. He was a difficult and irascible man, and he made the huge mistake of surrounding himself with yes-men. He sacked much of his best talent – or drove it away – for arguing with him or taking decisions without his approval. This meant that if he didn't spot danger coming, nobody else could make him see it. And he didn't see it until it was almost too late.

Ford was so convinced of the benefits of his Model T that he didn't bring out any other model until 1927, by which time Alfred P. Sloan was steering General Motors towards the biggest share of the market. Ford had to lay off his workers and shut down his plant for six months while he designed the replacement car, the Model A. But General Motors had the advantage and steamed into the lead in 1931, a position it has held ever since.

Ford's business was largely saved from collapse by World War II, when it began making bombers and jeeps. By then, Ford's image was tarnished, and all the more so by his controversial anti-Semitic views which he had expressed openly in his newspaper, *The Dearborn Independent*. Eventually, in 1945, his wife and daughter-in-law forced Ford to hand over his business to his grandson, Henry Ford II, who rescued the business and restored it at least to the number two spot in the car manufacturing stakes, where it still remains.

Ford may have failed to finish with quite the promise he started with, but his legacy to America – and beyond – was enormous. He created the first mass market, and invented mass production to satisfy it. He invented the moving assembly line and complete vertical integration. He contributed massively to the oil industry, to the road construction industry and to mass home ownership and the American middle class. If business leaders can be measured by their impact on wider society and culture, Ford is a tough act to beat.

BILL GATES

1955 –

Organisation: *Microsoft*

Key idea: *Hire, and keep, very smart people*

'The only big companies that succeed will be those that obsolete their own products before somebody else does.'

T he world's richest man. That's the epithet by which Gates is best known. A modern Rockefeller, he has amassed wealth on a scale never previously seen by being one of the very first with a vision of where the technological age could lead. His famously derided prediction of 'a computer on every desktop and in every home' has long since proved an accurate vision. But Gates wasn't the only geek around even back in the 1970s. So how come he ended up on top of the pile?

For a start, he had brains, with an especial talent for maths. He wrote his first computer program at the age of 13 and, together with his friend Paul Allen, wrote a scheduling program for their school. Soon afterwards, Gates and Allen founded a company that analysed city traffic data. But Gates didn't foresee a career in computers; he was going to Harvard to become a lawyer like his father.

However, in 1974, his friend Allen showed Gates the cover of a magazine carrying a picture of the MITS Altair 8800 – the very first PC. A computer anyone could build, it lacked only a keyboard, monitor and software. Gates and Allen got in touch with the manufacturers and offered to write a version of BASIC for the Altair. Their offer was accepted and – like Edwin Land over 40 years before – Gates quit Harvard to set up in business. He and Allen set up a company they called Microsoft, and business went well for a few years. Then came their big break. In 1980, IBM asked Gates to supply an operating system for its first personal computer. Gates response was to buy a ready-made system from another company, change its name to MS-DOS, and supply it to IBM.

Bill Gates ... on complacency

In this business, by the time you realise you're in trouble, it's too late to save yourself. Unless you're running scared all the time, you're gone.

This was the first point at which Gates, who had already demonstrated his considerable intelligence and technical ability, showed that he was a canny businessman, too. He didn't sell the operating system to IBM, he licensed it. As a result, Microsoft still gets a percentage from every IBM machine sold.

Microsoft continued to provide software, and developed consumer applications such as Microsoft Word. By 1986, when Microsoft went public, Gates was worth over a billion dollars. And that was just the start. Microsoft introduced its Windows software, and in the mid-1990s moved onto the Internet with its Internet Explorer browser.

Other organisations – and even customers – were by now beginning to complain that Microsoft had an effective monopoly. A string of legal battles followed, and in 1999 Microsoft was told (like John D. Rockefeller's Standard Oil in 1911) that it must be broken up into smaller companies.

The story sounds pretty impressive, but it still doesn't really explain how Gates succeeded ahead of all those other computer nerds playing with PCs back in the 1970s and early 1980s. The answer really lies in Gates' extraordinary mix of talents. Sure, he's a brainy computer type. But he's also a consummate dealer and businessman. He is highly competitive, and this is part of what drove him to buy out dozens of smaller companies and snowball them into the expanding Microsoft enterprise. His sometimes ruthless approach to business may have earned him criticism, but it also earned him big bucks.

Microsoft's programmers weren't doing anything that was more technologically advanced than other programmers, but Gates saw that the future lay in personal computers, and that ordinary people would want accessible software. His is not the most streamlined or the most technologically impressive software – but it is the easiest to use. And with Gates' vision of a computer on every desktop and in every home, he could see from the start that that was going to be more important than being sleek or clever.

Gates' vision went further than that, too. He created a new kind of computer organisation. He wasn't manufacturing hardware like everybody else – churning out keyboards or monitors – but creating a busi-

---

Bill Gates ... on marketing

If you can't make it good, make it look good.

---

ness founded entirely on intellectual property. Microsoft was the first software company.

So Gates was a technical genius and a corporate visionary. But that's still not all. He also turned out to be a skilled organisational manager. He recognised the need to take on talented people to help him run the organisation, and he knew how to recognise them. He says, 'There is no way of getting around that, in terms of IQ, you've got to be very elitist in picking the people who deserve to write software.' What's more – in an industry where people are by far the most valuable asset, and are frequently seduced by other companies – he knew how to hold onto them. He maximised job satisfaction, making sure his top people had all the tools they needed, and giving them as much scope as possible so that they felt in control of what they were doing.

And another key factor in Gates' management style: Microsoft pioneered the practice of giving stock options to all its employees, not just top management. This has made millionaires of literally thousands of Microsoft employees, and billionaires of a few of them. And, of course, it has done wonders for staff loyalty.

Since the legal disputes over Microsoft, Gates has stepped down as CEO and now fills the roles of chairman and chief software architect. He plans – following again in the footsteps of John D. Rockefeller – to give away most of his personal fortune, and has set up a foundation with an endowment of over $17 billion.

While Gates is never likely to be short of a bob or two, he has always maintained that the future of Microsoft cannot be certain. Numerous smaller organisations are working to break the Microsoft stranglehold on software systems and, as Gates knows, Microsoft has to keep running to stand still. But Gates has already managed his organisation through phenomenal growth – at times as high as 600 per cent a year – and if anyone has the leadership skills to keep his organisation at the top of the pile, he does.

HAROLD GENEEN

1910–1997

Organisation: *ITT*

Key idea: *Watch the balance sheet*

'Management is not a collection of boxes with names and titles on the organisational chart. Management is a living force.'

H arold Geneen was the archetypical American manager: bullish and overbearing, he believed in hard work and management by facts and figures. His enormous talent enabled him to build ITT into a giant of a conglomerate. However, he created a teetering pile of diverse companies, which – without his hand to keep it steady – soon fell apart after he left. No one else, apparently, could do what he did.

Geneen was born in England, but moved to America when he was less than a year old. He was always good with numbers, and earned a degree in accountancy from New York University. He then took accounting jobs and applied what would be his lifelong principles of hard work and an instinct for facts and figures. Geneen worked his way up through American Can Co., Bell & Howell and Jones & Laughlin. Eventually he joined Raytheon as executive vice president, where he turned around the company's fortunes.

After three years at Raytheon, the company was taken over by ITT, a disparate group of mostly international businesses vaguely centred on the telecommunications industry (the initials ITT stand for International Telephone and Telegraph). Geneen took over at the helm of ITT in 1959. His mission: to turn it into the world's biggest conglomerate.

Conglomerating businesses was one of the great management obsessions of the 1960s, and Geneen turned out to be the master at it. In his view, diversification meant strength, so he began to buy up companies at an unprecedented rate, with no concern about the products so long as

Harold Geneen ... on leadership

Leadership is practised not so much in words as in attitude and in actions.

they were profitable. Geneen said the only industries he wouldn't enter were chemicals, movies and airlines.

Geneen acquired 350 companies in the next ten years or so, operating in 70 countries, and as diverse as Avis Rent-A-Car, Sheraton Hotels, the insurer Hartford, and bread maker Continental Baking. He once commented, 'Will Rogers said he never met a man he didn't like. Well, I never met a business that I didn't find interesting.' Geneen was indeed captivated by business, being famously workaholic and with little time for socialising.

His strategy certainly worked for ITT. When Geneen took over, annual sales were around $765 million. Under his direction, this figure grew to $22 billion. Managing this huge organisation was an extraordinarily complex operation, and Geneen believed in hiring the best people. He had no time for flashy managers but preferred hard working, hard-headed men like himself: 'We set out to hire the very best people in the industry that we could find. I did not want glamorous, glib-talking men who got by on their coiffured good looks or family connections.'

Once Geneen had appointed talented people, there were few perks in the job, either. He insisted: 'All these ego-feeding activities – the long hours in the limousine, the skylarking in the corporate jet, the collection of press clippings, the unnecessary speeches – feed the corporate sickness and one way or another make a corporate problem out of what had been an otherwise perfectly competent, even brilliant executive.' Geneen was not known for his sense of fun.

What he was known for was his control of facts and figures. He was more on top of his vast empire than seems possible. He spent his time poring over reports and balance sheets; he was always an accountant at heart. He constantly checked up on his managers, and had a reputation for cross-examining them bluntly. One of his key management tools was to hold frequent management meetings, including a monthly meeting which ITT managers from around the world would attend to give progress reports on their businesses.

Factual analysis was at the heart of Geneen's management style, and he claimed, 'The highest art of professional management requires the literal ability to "smell" a "real fact" from all others.' Geneen used

Harold Geneen … on financial figures

When you have mastered numbers, you will in fact no longer be reading numbers, any more than you read words when reading books. You will be reading meanings.

logic to run his business, not instinct (except, perhaps, the instinct for smelling out a fact). He described it as, 'the business logic that results in making decisions which are almost inevitable because all the facts on which the decisions must be based are available.'

Geneen's relentless style and his forceful personality, coupled with his brilliant ability to think analytically and to juggle control of all ITT's separate businesses, kept the conglomerate growing right through the sixties and into the seventies. Geneen stepped down as CEO in 1977 and as chairman of the board in 1979. The workaholic couldn't retire, though, and continued working – creating several small companies – until his death nearly twenty years later, at the age of 87.

It wasn't long after Geneen retired from ITT that it began to crumble and collapse. Eventually the conglomerate was largely dismantled and many of the businesses sold off. Geneen's explanation was, 'After I left, the company veered on to a new course, emphasising consolidation rather than growth.' But it wasn't just that. Geneen had managed to keep literally hundreds of balls in the air throughout his leadership but no one else could juggle like he could. In the end the one failure of his leadership was that he had achieved that incredibly rare thing: he had made himself indispensable.

16

LEW GRADE

1906–1998

Organisation: *ATV (Associated Television)*

Key idea: *Give the public what they want*

'What's two plus two? Am I buying or selling?'

L
ew Grade was one of the biggest characters in the entertainments industry in 20th-century Britain, more in the mould of a Hollywood mogul than a UK television executive. He came from an immigrant Russian family that settled in London's East End and he became the first and biggest figure in commercial television – a medium that didn't take off until he was nearly 50 years old.

By the time television lured Grade to become a producer, he had already built up an impressive, and remarkably varied, career. As Louis Winogradsky, he arrived in England at the age of six and immediately launched into a successful school career – notably in mathematics – which was cut short when his family decided he'd be better off learning a trade. So he left school at 15 to work in the rag trade. He promptly discovered his tremendous flair for business, and by the time he was 16 he was setting up his own clothing company in Aldgate. Business thrived, and Grade worked long hours to make it successful.

But he managed to find time for leisure, too, and was caught up in the craze for the Charleston dance, which swept the country in the early 1920s. Grade was a talented dancer, and the Charleston came so naturally to him that he picked up prize after prize, eventually becoming Charleston Champion of the World in 1926. His dance act became so popular that he toured Europe, and then joined the English music hall circuit. By now he had left the rag trade behind in favour of the entertainment business. And he had changed his name to Lew Grade.

By 1934, the physical strain of performing was starting to show, and Grade's performances often left him in great pain. So he opted for another career change. He had a talent for spotting popular acts, and had often recommended performers he'd seen to a booking agent named Joe Collins (father of the actress Joan Collins). All his recommendations were excellent, and Collins had taken them all on. So Grade figured he'd try to become a booking agent himself.

His eye for a good act, along with his innate business skills, earned him a strong reputation and before long Joe Collins offered him a partnership. By now, Grade was making quite a name for himself as a talent spotter and he and Collins decided to put on their own shows as well as providing artists for other people's. Their plans were interrupted initially by the war, but Grade soon began providing entertainment for the troops. When his younger brother Leslie was called up, Grade left his partnership with Collins to run Leslie's booking agency for him.

Grade was nervous of some of the big clients on his brother's books, including Val Parnell, who ran the Stoll Moss Theatres Group. To help Grade overcome his nerves, his wife Kathie bought him a box of cigars and suggested he offer them to his clients to create a more relaxed atmosphere. Grade had never tried a cigar, and wondered what they were like. One day, as he related later, 'I opened the box, pulled out a cigar, cut off the tip (as I'd often seen people do) and lit up. It just so happened that, precisely at the moment I was taking my first couple of puffs, and enjoying it enormously, the telephone rang. It was Val Parnell. "Yes, Val," I said, cigar in hand, and no longer intimidated by this formidable man, "what can I do for you?" That was the day the real Lew Grade was born.'

After the war, Grade and his brother Leslie formed a company together, and Lew took his talent-spotting skills – along with his business acumen – to America and came back with acts such as Abbot and Costello, Jack Benny and Judy Garland. By now, Grade was making important contacts and mixing with highly influential people in the entertainments industry. He was also earning respect not least for being a man of his word – many of Grade's best deals never made it onto paper, because everyone knew they could trust him.

That was Lew Grade's career until commercial television arrived in the mid 1950s. Already impressive, it was nothing to what it would become as he capitalised on the new medium. When the franchises for the new ITV territories came up in the UK, the initial capital requirement for each was £3 million – out of Grade's league. Until, that is, one of his client's managers called him up and told him that if he could put

Lew Grade ... on grasping opportunities

You can't wait for the phone to ring. You have to phone them.

together a sufficiently distinguished board, and find £1 million, he had a backer who would put up the other £2 million.

Grade spent an hour on the phone, at the end of which he had put together a board that included the top theatre producers in the country, as well as the right hand man of John Schlesinger, the South African millionaire who owned (among other things) a chain of cinemas. It was typical of Grade's energetic style of business. But there was a problem. One of his recruits to the board was Val Parnell who phoned Grade back to say that his boss, Prince Littler, who owned Stoll Moss Theatre Group, was totally opposed to television and wouldn't let Parnell have anything to do with it. Grade turned on the legendary salesmanship and went to visit Littler. By the end of the day he had not only persuaded him of the virtues of television, but talked him into becoming chairman of the new company as well as a major backer.

The irony was that Grade's team was so impressive, including as it did representatives of the top producers of the time, that the new company was refused a franchise on the grounds that it would have a monopoly on the British entertainments industry.

Undeterred by this failed bid, Grade and his backers instead formed an independent production company to make programmes for the new commercial franchises, starting with *The Adventures of Robin Hood*. ITC (the Independent Television Corporation) later joined with one of the franchise companies to form ATV (Associated Television), the production company that dominated commercial television throughout the next two decades.

Grade was made for commercial television. He had a natural instinct for the kind of programming the public wanted to watch, he had an eye for talent, and he was a terrific salesman. His company produced successes such as *The Saint, The Prisoner, Thunderbirds, Coronation Street* and *The Muppet Show*. Grade became Chairman of ITC and was knighted and, eventually, given a life peerage for his services to the entertainments industry. But it didn't stop at television. Grade became one of the very few successful British movie producers of the time, with films such as *Return of the Pink Panther, The Eagle Has Landed, The Muppet Movie* and *Sophie's Choice*. However, it wasn't all success; Grade was forced to sell his company in 1982 after famously losing a fortune on the film *Raise*

Lew Grade ... on selling

When the phone doesn't ring at home I get depressed. So my wife says, 'Why not go out and sell something, Lew?' And that always cheers me up.

---

the Titanic. As he said himself, 'It would have been cheaper to lower the Atlantic.'

Grade didn't retire however – despite being well into his 70s – but became chairman of Embassy Communications and then formed his own company, The Grade Company. He eventually died at the age of 91; up until his final short illness he was still displaying the enormous energy and enthusiasm that had driven him all his life – like so many of the most inspirational leaders. Asked what he would like his epitaph to be, he once said: 'It will be "I didn't want to go. And I'm not going."'

ALFRED HARMSWORTH (LORD NORTHCLIFFE)

1865–1922

Organisation: *Times Newspapers*

Key idea: *Popularising the daily press*

'News is what somebody somewhere wants to suppress. All the rest is advertising.'

Alfred Harmsworth was one of the great newspaper magnates of the first half of the 20th century, the contemporary of Max Aitken (Lord Beaverbrook). His career – from journalist to press baron – was founded on his extraordinary ability to judge what people wanted to read and his innovative approach to his industry. He is recognised as the creator of the popular daily press.

After an undistinguished school career – apart from editing the school magazine – Harmsworth went straight into journalism as a writer and then an editor. However, he soon decided to launch his own magazine in partnership with his brother. The most popular magazine of the time was called *Tit-Bits*, and the Harmsworths reckoned they could compete with their new publication, *Answers to Correspondents*. It was a huge success and topped a million copies a week after four years. Harmsworth ploughed much of his profit into launching other publications.

Having established his talent for identifying what readers wanted, Harmsworth decided to try his hand at newspaper publishing. So in 1894 he bought a failing newspaper, *The Evening News*, and radically overhauled it. He kept the basic format, but reduced the advertising and put more emphasis on news, introducing catchy headlines such as 'Hypnotism and Lunacy', and 'Was it Suicide or Apoplexy?' By the end of the year, this popular approach had turned around the newspaper's fortunes, and sales were approaching 400,000 a day. If only they owned more printing presses, Harmsworth claimed, sales would top half a million. Two years later, circulation was closer to 800,000.

Again, Harmsworth used his profits to launch another newspaper. He took the type of newspaper popular in the US as a model: simpler and more readable than the daily papers already available. And he added innovations of his own: he invented the banner headline that went right across the page, and he included a section especially for women. He gave plenty of space to sport, and to stories of human interest. What's more, he charged only a halfpenny for his new daily, while others were priced at one penny. He called his new paper the *Daily Mail*. It launched in May 1896, and he hoped it would sell 100,000 copies on its first day but he was wrong. It sold 400,000.

In fact, Harmsworth's timing couldn't have been better for launching a popular daily newspaper. Only a few years earlier it would have been impossible, but several factors had come together to make it feasible. One of these was the national rail network, which made it possible to distribute what would be a million copies a day before the end of the century. The new technology was a huge help too, enabling Harmsworth to print such large runs. And the other factor was the mass literacy that had resulted from educational reforms over the previous 20 years: newspapers had been for the educated few who could read them. Now Harmsworth opened the medium up to the masses from almost all classes who had become literate.

There was never any question, from the day of its launch, that the *Daily Mail* would be a huge hit. As sales climbed (boosted by popular interest in the Boer War in 1899), Harmsworth's reputation grew. Joseph Pulitzer asked him to edit the *New York World*, which he did. He started by changing its size to a smaller format, which he christened 'tabloid'.

Not only did Harmsworth bring new ideas to publishing, he also promoted innovation. He publicised the virtues of electric light, the telephone, photography and aeroplanes. In fact he was such a fan of the new motor car that he banned his editor at the *Daily Mail* from reporting car accidents.

Harmsworth decided it was time to launch yet another new kind of daily paper. He believed there was a market for a daily aimed specifically at women. So in 1903 he invested hugely in his latest venture, the *Daily Mirror*. First day sales were excellent but the circulation soon dropped off, and the paper began to lose big money. It was Harmsworth's biggest failure. He said, 'Some people say that a woman never really knows what she wants. It is certain she knew what she didn't want. She didn't want the *Daily Mirror*.'

Alfred Harmsworth on … accepting failure

The faculty of knowing when you are beaten is much more valuable than the faculty of thinking you are not beaten when you are.

But he wasn't beaten. He halved the price and filled the newspaper full of photographs and pictures, aimed at men as well as women. Pioneering the use of pictures in the press (which he soon introduced to the *Daily Mail* too), Harmsworth published a whole page of pictures of Edward VII and his children. It was a massive success. The press had discovered the public's enduring fascination with pictures of their royal family, and the *Daily Mirror* was back on track – albeit a slightly different track.

Among Harmsworth's next innovations were the exclusive interview, and the idea of sponsoring events. The *Daily Mirror* offered a hundred guineas in 1904 for the first person to swim the English Channel. Thanks to his fascination with new inventions, Harmsworth offered another prize in 1906, this time £1000 for the first airman to fly across the Channel, and £10,000 for the first to fly from London to Manchester. He was widely derided for imagining such achievements possible, but his faith in new technology was rewarded. By 1910 he had awarded both his prizes.

In 1904, Harmsworth was offered a baronetcy, having previously turned down a knighthood. And in 1905 he became the youngest peer of the realm ever when he took the title Lord Northcliffe. His enemies accused him of purchasing his title corruptly, since he had said in the past, 'When I want a peerage, I will buy one honestly.'

Northcliffe's next step in building his press empire was to buy the *Sunday Observer* and, in 1908, the ailing *Times* newspaper. His popular touch – and readiness to drop the price – soon turned these newspapers into successful publications alongside the *Mail* and the *Mirror.*

Northcliffe now controlled most of what was read in the papers around the country, and war was looming. It put him in a position of great power; a position which made the government extremely nervous. Northcliffe was outspoken and used his newspapers to promote his own political views. He had long been predicting war with Germany, and was viewed as a warmonger by many people.

Northcliffe made sure that the *Daily Mail* was the newspaper read by the army. He arranged for 10,000 copies of it to be delivered to the

---

Alfred Harmsworth on … journalism

A profession whose business it is to explain to others what it personally does not understand.

Western Front each day, and he had yet another of his new ideas. He
would pay front line soldiers for articles about their experiences.

It wasn't long before the government's fears about Northcliffe were
realised. He criticised Lord Kitchener, and claimed that thanks to him
the army didn't have the right kind of high-explosive shell to defend
itself. Her argued that men were dying needlessly thanks to Kitchener's failure. His comments upset a lot of people and circulation of the
Daily Mail dropped drastically. But it didn't stop him. He also attacked
the government for the failure at Gallipoli, and criticised its overall war
strategy.

By 1916 Northcliffe was campaigning to remove Herbert Asquith
as Prime Minister, claiming that the Germans were far more afraid of
Lloyd George becoming PM. In the end, Northcliffe got what he wanted
and Asquith resigned. Lloyd George could see that, much as he disliked Northcliffe, the only safe place to have him was in the cabinet.
But Northcliffe could see it too, and turned down the invitation on the
grounds that he would be unable to criticise the government. Deeply
frustrated, Lloyd George said privately that Northcliffe was 'one of the
biggest intriguers and most unscrupulous people in the country.'

However, in March 1918, Northcliffe was finally persuaded to join
the government by Lord Beaverbrook, owner of the *Daily Express* and
Minister of Information. Northcliffe took charge of propaganda directed at enemy countries. But he resigned his post on Armistice Day, and
refused to support Lloyd George's government.

Although Northcliffe's interest in new technology persisted after
the war – he campaigned heavily to promote wireless communication –
his health soon deteriorated and he died in 1922. He left three months'
salary to every one of his employees in his will – all six thousand of them.
But his greatest legacy was his invention of the popular daily newspaper.

WILLIAM RANDOLPH HEARST

1863–1951

Organisation: *The Hearst Corporation*

Key idea: *Popularising the press*

'You provide the pictures. I'll provide the war.'

William Randolph Hearst's story is a classic riches to riches tale. Nevertheless, despite a wealthy background, he still managed to exceed all possible expectations and made his father's multimillions look like mere pocket money. Like many of his most successful contemporaries, he saw the potential in the new communications technologies, from print media to films, and knew how to make them popular.

Hearst was undoubtedly a genius when it came to communicating with the public, and an inspirational business leader. But he was not a popular personality. The thinly veiled and unflattering account of his life in Orson Welles' 1941 film *Citizen Kane* is reckoned to be a fairly accurate depiction. He was considered an authoritarian megalomaniac, obsessed with power and status. He was even credited with starting the Spanish-American War in 1898 in order to boost the circulation of his newspapers.

Hearst's background was a privileged one. His father, George Hearst, was a miner and rancher, and a self-made multimillionaire. In 1880, George Hearst was given the *San Francisco Examiner*, a small daily newspaper, in lieu of a gambling debt. He kept the newspaper ticking over and his son, meanwhile, became a student at Harvard University. But William Randolph Hearst decided he wanted to run the newspaper himself, and wrote to his father from Harvard: 'I am convinced that I could run a newspaper successfully. Now, if you should make over to me the *Examiner*, with enough money to carry out my schemes ...' After some persuasion George Hearst agreed to his son's idea and, in March

1887, William Randolph Hearst became owner of the newspaper, at the age of 23.

Hearst immediately started putting in long hours and working hard to improve the circulation of his newspaper. He upgraded his equipment, improved relationships with advertisers, and overhauled the look of the newspaper. And he hired in some of the best journalists around. He gave the content more sense of purpose, with stories of corruption and campaigns for civic improvements. He called his paper 'The Monarch of the Dailies'.

Hearst's improvements brought higher circulation and an enviable reputation for his newspaper, and he was enthused by his success. In 1895, he moved to New York and bought the *New York Journal*. His empire had been born. Next up was the *Chicago American*, followed by a string of newspapers in cities across America. By 1905 Hearst started adding magazines to his portfolio, beginning with *Motor*, a publication inspired by his honeymoon drive across Europe. Among the titles he added to this – and which are still owned by the Hearst Corporation – were *Cosmopolitan* and *Good Housekeeping*.

Hearst's newspapers were a huge success – at one time they were read by a quarter of all Americans – thanks to his popular and innovative brand of journalism. Like Lord Northcliffe, his contemporary across the Atlantic, Hearst knew how to make newspapers appealing to the public. The style of journalism he promoted was energetic and forceful, with plenty of short, punchy pieces. He was prepared to pay well over the odds for top-class reporters to ensure high-quality news output, and particularly delighted in luring top staff away from his arch-rival, Joseph Pulitzer. Hearst's newspapers used illustrations, photographs and catchy layouts, and he was the first newspaper publisher to use colour printing, halftone photographs, and colour comic sections. Hearst was also the first to syndicate news copy, selling stories from around the world to other newspapers.

Hearst was famous for the guidelines he laid down for his editors and journalists, to ensure that all his newspapers followed the Hearst style. His approach was to make articles brief, simple and compelling, and his rules for achieving this (some of which are set out below) are as relevant today as they were a hundred years ago.

By the 1920s, other communication media were starting to take off, and Hearst played a pioneering role. He began to shoot news footage on film all around the world and launched his new company, Hearst Metrotone News, in 1929 to an enthusiastic reception. He also bought up radio stations across the US, and even owned the very first television station, launched just a few years before his death.

> ## William Randolph Hearst ... on what constitutes news
>
> News is largely a matter of what one man wants the people to know and feel and think.

William Randolph Hearst was also famous for his political aspirations. Although he was elected to the House of Representatives twice, he failed in his bid to become governor of New York State in 1906. Nevertheless, he took a great interest in politics and in promoting his views through his newspapers, and was proud of his claim of having started a war virtually singlehandedly; one of the chief events that earned him his infamous reputation for the callous pursuit of power and profit.

The war in question was the Spanish–American war, which many people believed would never happen, and could be avoided. But Hearst wanted it to happen; he knew it would sell newspapers. He published inflammatory articles in his newspapers to fan the flames, and it is popularly reckoned that the war might never have happened without him. Certainly his reputation was sealed by the cable he sent his artist Frederic Remington. Hearst had despatched Remington to Cuba with a brief to cover the anticipated war. After a few days Remington wired Hearst: 'Everything is quiet. There is no trouble here. There will be no war. I wish to return.' Hearst cabled back: 'Please remain. You provide the pictures. I'll provide the war.'

Hearst was a hugely influential figure, despite his limited political success, and was a close friend and advisor to many leading opinion politicians and opinion makers. By the time he died in 1951, he had built the Hearst Corporation up into a massive industry, which has continued to grow. Today it employs 16,000 people employed in over a hundred businesses. And Hearst's guidelines for writing articles which people will want to read are still central to the organisation.

William Randolph Hearst's guidelines for editors (1933)

- Make a paper for the nicest kind of people – for the great middle class. Don't print a lot of dull stuff people are supposed to like and don't.
- Please be accurate. Don't allow exaggeration. It is a cheap and ineffective substitute for real interest. Reward reporters who make the truth interesting, and weed out those who don't.

William Randolph Hearst ... on satisfying customers

Papers are made more readable by brief articles ... We are not making short stories to save money, we are making them to save readers... We are doing the work. Our readers are not paid to work; we are.

- Make the news thorough. Print all the news. Condense it if necessary. Frequently it is better when intelligently condensed. But get it in.
- Omit things that will offend nice people. Avoid coarseness and a low tone. The most sensational news can be told if told properly.
- Make your headlines clear and concise statements of interesting acts ... Don't allow copyreaders to write headlines that are too smart or too clever to be intelligible.
- Nothing is more wearisome than mere words. Have our people tell stories briefly and pointedly.
- Please instruct copyreaders to rewrite long sentences into several short ones. And please try to educate the reporters to write short sentences in the first place.
- Make every picture worth its space.
- If you cannot show conclusively your own paper's superiority, you may be sure the public will never discover it.

HENRY J. HEINZ
1844–1919

Organisation: *H J Heinz*

Key idea: *Improving employee conditions*

'Quality is to a product what character is to a man.'

H enry John Heinz was one of those natural entrepreneurs who cannot help but succeed. Not only was he blessed with the qualities he needed to build a remarkable business, but he was also one of the world's great philanthropists. His spirit of care for employees and for others survives in the company to this day.

From the age of eight, Heinz was finding ways to make money, by selling off surplus home-grown vegetables to his family's neighbours. By the time he was 16, his deliveries to local grocers in his home town of Pittsburgh, Pennsylvania, were filling three wagons a week.

In 1869, at the age of 24, Heinz started his first company, Heinz and Noble, together with his friend L. Clarence Noble. Their first product was grated horseradish from his mother's garden, bottled in clear glass so that its quality could be judged. Heinz and Noble did well until 1875, when the business went bankrupt. However, Heinz wasn't going to give up that easily, and the following year he launched a new company to-gether with his brother and cousin, which they called the F & J Heinz Company.

This time they had a new product: tomato ketchup. Their range also included other condiments and pickles, jams and jellies. The busi-ness was a big success, and soon Heinz was expanding into new land for growing and new buildings for preparation of his products. Heinz insisted his goods were made from only the best ingredients, freshly picked and checked for quality. He was also adamant that his factories should be spotlessly clean – in fact he was so proud of his hygiene stand-ards that he invented the public factory tour to show them off.

Henry J. Heinz ... on advertising

It's not so much what you say, but how, when and where.

In 1888 the business was restructured and renamed the H J Heinz Company. Heinz not only had a talent for running the business, he was also a born salesman and advertiser, and was famous for displaying the Heinz name on billboards and in newspapers and magazines. He devised many successful advertising slogans, the most famous being '57 varieties'. Heinz was on a business trip to New York when he saw an ad for a shoe store which proclaimed the huge range of shoes it stocked. This impressed him so much that he decided to try the same approach himself. The number 57 simply came into his head as the one to use, although H J Heinz already had far more than 57 varieties.

Heinz was a canny businessman too, and by 1900 he had salesman in every continent selling H J Heinz products. He established farms across America and abroad as well, both for convenience in preparation and selling and also so that if the crop should fail anywhere he had plenty of backup sources of supply. (By the time he died in 1916 he had over 100,000 acres of farmland.)

One of Heinz's business advantages was the great love and loyalty he earned from his employees, and it is his inspiring leadership for which he is arguably best remembered. The working conditions for H J Heinz employees often surpassed their living conditions. At his Pittsburgh factory he installed separate men's and women's bathrooms, a library, a roof garden, lunch rooms and a lecture hall where he often staged entertainments for his employees, hiring some of the top names.

Heinz also introduced many working practices which, for their time, were highly advanced. He believed that the way to keep workers happy and motivated was to make sure that their managers kept in close touch with them and their welfare. He used to impress on his heads of department that it was only by developing the staff under them that they themselves would develop, and he himself set the pattern by giving positive encouragement to all his employees. This led not only to high morale in the workforce, but also to an enormously strong sense of community which boosted morale even further.

Heinz was proud of the fact that there was never a workers' strike in his company, which he attributed to the fact that management were always in close and sympathetic touch with the workers (of whom there were over 4500 by the time he died). Heinz instituted daily meetings

Henry J. Heinz ... on motivation

Heart power is better than horse power.

at which younger representatives of the company, such as his own sons, would meet with heads of department to discuss their work. Not only that, but the meetings would also hear sympathetically from workers of any rank who wanted to make any suggestion or criticism. In addition to this, once a year all heads of department and foremen would meet to discuss the business.

Henry J. Heinz was a genuinely kind and generous man, and was deeply involved in his local community, giving generously to numerous causes. As he said, 'Make all you can honestly, save all you can prudently, give all you can wisely. He who enjoys the first two and deprives himself of the latter privilege, denies himself the greatest enjoyment of life.'

Heinz died of pneumonia in 1919 at the age of 74. His business remained a family-run firm for nearly a century, and was lucky enough to be headed by a succession of talented leaders, including his son and grandson. Its spirit of community and philanthropy remained, and Heinz was an early pioneer of environmental measures, from the first fully recyclable plastic ketchup bottle to the first dolphin-safe tuna. Heinz's company now markets over 5700 varieties of product in more than 200 countries.

HERB KELLEHER

1931–

Organisation: *Southwest Airlines*

Key idea: *Create a culture that attracts customers*

'The more time I spend with our people, the more I learn about our company.'

Herb Kelleher is a maverick. He likes to do things his own way, and doesn't care two hoots for convention. As it happens, his way of doing things is a pretty good way, and he has built his airline up into one of the most successful in the US. He is perhaps best known for his zany sense of fun, which permeates the culture of the whole organisation and makes it so immensely popular with its customers.

Despite the practical joker image, Kelleher is a smart businessman, who sailed through school, college and law school and then set up as a lawyer in San Antonio, Texas, in 1960. He continued to practise for several years, but in 1966 he had a conversation with one of his clients that would eventually launch him into a major career change. He was having a meeting in a bar with an entrepreneur named Rollin King, who told Kelleher that what he reckoned Texas needed was an inexpensive airline service to link its three biggest cities, Dallas, Houston and San Antonio. The two of them sketched out a flight pattern on a paper napkin (which is now framed in the offices of Southwest Airlines).

Kelleher was impressed with the idea, but Texas' three top airlines didn't like it all all, and set out to block Southwest Airlines' application for certification as an airline. In fact, for the next four years it cost Southwest over half a million dollars in legal bills to fight their case, and almost everyone behind the idea apart from Kelleher was ready to give up on it. But he insisted on a final appeal to the Texas Supreme Court. He won it.

Southwest Airlines started operating in 1971 with Kelleher as chief legal counsel. The president was an experienced airline executive called Lamar Muse. The first few years were extremely tough, as the competition still tried their best to put the new company out of business. But by its third year, the company was starting to make a profit. In 1978, Muse resigned, and Kelleher was asked to replace him.

Many might have seen Kelleher's inexperience in the airline industry as a weakness, but he turned it to his advantage. He took no notice of traditions or even fads in the industry, but took all his decisions on the twin principles of keeping costs down and customers happy. When other airlines switched to the 'hub' system of routing all flights through key, centrally placed airports, Kelleher didn't join in. He reckoned it was cheaper, and more convenient for passengers, to go on flying direct between cities.

Kelleher did everything he could to keep costs down, and to make Southwest's flights more affordable than anyone else's. He didn't want to compete with other airlines so much as with bus and coach companies. He realised that it was essential to cut down turnaround times on flights so as to pack in more journeys. To this end he abandoned designated seating to speed up boarding time: passengers are let on the plane in groups of 30, and they can pick their own seats on a first come, first served basis (all seats are standard class). Turnaround is also reduced by abandoning in-flight meals, since these take time to load and unload. It obviously reduces costs, too. Southwest Airlines famously serves only peanuts on its flights. In fact, Kelleher's airline can turn a flight around in as little as 20 minutes, less than half the average time of other airlines. And its costs are over 20 per cent below the industry average.

Southwest's service expanded well beyond Texas, and now serves well over 50 cities around the US. Travelling by Southwest isn't luxurious, but it's certainly cheap. Not only that, but Southwest consistently rates as the most profitable US airline, and earns the top rating for baggage handling and on-time performance. It also has the fewest customer complaints.

Kelleher's airline may have grown, but he still views it as a small-scale operation. He argues, 'Think small and act small, and we'll get bigger. Think big and act big, and we'll get smaller.' In fact, Southwest Airlines is now one of the biggest airlines in the US.

Kelleher claims he never makes long-term plans for his business. He says, 'If it's a plan, it ain't sincere and it doesn't work ... We don't even do one-year plans. When we bump up against some benchmark that requires us to make a major decision, we review our strategic definition of the airline and decide whether we should depart from it.'

Herb Kelleher ... on employees

Southwest has its customers, the passengers; and I have my customers, the airline's employees. If the passengers aren't satisfied, they won't fly with us. If the employees aren't satisfied, they won't provide the product we need.

Not only did Kelleher have no experience of the airline industry when he started out, he had no experience as a manager either. So he developed his own approach to dealing with people. He applied his eccentric style to his airline from the start, and soon earned a reputation for humour that is unparalleled inside or outside his industry. Whether you work for Southwest or whether you're a customer, the aim is that the experience should be fun. Kelleher maintains that this culture has to begin with his staff.

At Southwest's headquarters, everyone wears casual clothes, and there is frequent fooling around and practical joking. It's actively encouraged, as are the celebrations, birthday parties and awards that punctuate work time at the office. Good performance is praised publicly in the company newsletter and the in-flight magazine. Kelleher has extremely high recruitment standards, and looks for staff with a sense of humour: 'We don't care that much about education and expertise, because we can train people to do whatever they have to do. We hire attitudes.'

Employees are actively encouraged to be individual and to give the best service to customers no matter what. It is enshrined in official company policy that 'No employee will ever be punished for using good judgement and good old common sense when trying to accommodate a customer – no matter what our other rules are.'

Southwest Airlines has the most unionised workforce in the industry; Kelleher is pro-union. And yet it has never lost a single hour as a result of a workforce dispute. Kelleher's individual management style seems to pre-empt trouble. On one occasion, Southwest's flight schedulers nearly came to blows with the flight attendants over the schedules. Kelleher's response was to get them to swap jobs for a day to see the issue from each other's perspective. Kelleher, or Uncle Herb as his employees refer to him, gets a massively high level of loyalty from his staff, who often work extra hours for nothing in order to give good service to customers.

Herb Kelleher ... on customers

The customer is frequently wrong. We don't carry those sorts of customers. We write them and say, 'Fly somebody else. Don't abuse our people.'

Kelleher's eccentricity is legendary, and his sense of humour inspires his staff. On one occasion, he settled a dispute with another airline's CEO over the rights to a particular slogan by arm-wrestling him for it. On another occasion, while addressing a group of Wall Streeters, he declared his two greatest achievements: a talent for projectile vomiting, and never having had a really serious venereal disease.

It would be impossible for such an infectious sense of fun not to spread to the customers, and of course it does. Flying Southwest Airlines is fun. Customers don't just come for the cheap flights, they also come to wind down at the end of a tough day, to feel special, to have a laugh. Flight attendants have been known to sing the safety instructions as a rap or as country music, and to dress up as leprechauns on St Patrick's day. They organise games from peanut-catching to seeing how many passengers can fit into the toilet at one time. In-flight announcements have been known to include: 'Will those of you who wish to smoke please file out to our lounge on the wing, where you can enjoy our feature movie, *Gone with the Wind.*'

And Kelleher's personal approach also means that every letter of complaint is personally answered, regular customers are recognised and treated as friends, and the organisation is always ready to make changes if it benefits the passengers. Southwest has an enviable record of customer loyalty.

Herb Kelleher has turned humour into a hugely valuable commodity. His combination of low prices, top quality service and fun, fun, fun is a reflection of his pragmatic and warm personality. And no one has yet managed to copy it. As Kelleher explains: 'It's interesting when folks come to Southwest Airlines from some other company. They visit us, and then they want to establish a culture similar to ours. When you tell them it's just treating people right, that's too simplistic for them. They want something far more complex. They want a program. We always felt that making it a program murders it.

PHIL KNIGHT
1938–
Organisation: *Nike*

Key idea: *Manufacturing overseas to cut costs*

'There is no value in making things any more. The value is added by careful research, by innovation and by marketing.'

N ike is one of the few truly global brands, a multibillion dollar business selling sports shoes, designed to give the competition a run for its money. Its emphasis on innovation and continuous improvement has earned the company market leader position. The business was the brainchild of its founder, Phil Knight, an exemplary exponent of the company's famous slogan 'Just do it'.

Knight grew up in Portland, Oregon, and was a keen sportsman from the start. At the University of Oregon, where he studied accounting, he was a mile runner, with a personal best of 4 minutes 10 seconds. He continued to run while attending Stanford University for his MBA, which is where he and his coach started selling sports shoes.

His work for his MBA was what gave him the first glimmer of an idea for starting a business selling running shoes. At the time, the market was dominated by expensive, German-made shoes. Knight reckoned that shoes could be designed in the US but manufactured in Japan, where costs were lower, before being shipped back to America to sell at lower prices than the competition.

So Knight and his coach, Bob Bowerman, began importing Japanese running shoes and adding their own brand name – Blue Ribbon Sports. They sold their sports shoes to local track runners out of the back of a car. Business was reasonable, but not good enough to give up the day job. So Knight worked teaching accounting at Portland State University while he ran his shoe importing business on the side.

> ## Phil Knight ... on mistakes
>
> The trouble in America is not that we are making too many mistakes, but that we are making too few.

One day, when Knight was expecting a delegation of Japanese businessman to visit in a few days, he met a graphic design student in the corridor at the University. Her name was Carolyn Davidson. Knight asked her to help him prepare some charts and graphs for the visit. He was pleased with the results, so he offered her $35 to come up with a shoe stripe for the company logo in time for the Japanese visit. His only brief was that it should give the impression of movement. Davidson produced a selection of designs, none of which impressed Knight hugely. However, he was pressed for time, so he picked one, reckoning it would grow on him. It was the 'swoosh' sign that has come to be recognised around the world as the Nike symbol.

In 1972, Knight produced his first running shoes under the Nike brand name, which he picked because Nike was the Greek goddess of victory. He realised that jogging was just becoming fashionable, so he targeted his shoes at non-professional runners too. Suddenly, the company's prospects began to improve dramatically. Before long, trainers became a fashion statement, and Knight was selling his shoes to everyone, from children to grandparents.

By the end of the 1970s, Nike had half the US market and a turnover of around $150 million. Its growth was due to Knight's determination to improve continuously, and keep building new and innovative features into the product such as the waffle sole, introduced in 1975. Nike has always invested heavily in long-term research and development. Knight and his company have a reputation as the bad boys of the industry, with an aggressive marketing style and an irreverence for any kind of sporting authority.

Massive advertising campaigns, headed up by big sports stars, are another Nike hallmark. Nike's annual advertising budget is around $200 million. Athletes such as Tiger Woods and André Agassi endorse Nike products – personalities who are globally recognised champions, and who also share some of the Nike image of being not quite establishment figures in the sporting world.

The only time Nike lost its place as market leader was in the 1980s when it was slow to recognise the emerging market for women's aerobic shoes, and was beaten into second place by Reebok. Nike responded

Phil Knight ... on business atmosphere

It's my job to create an atmosphere of peace in the chaos of business – something I've learnt from Asian business style.

successfully with a combination of innovation and big-name advertising, as usual: basketball superstar Michael Jordan endorsed the 'Air Jordan' shoe and Nike was back on top of the pile.

Knight is a quietly charismatic figure, almost never seen publicly without his trademark Nike shades. He is still a sports fanatic, and staff at Nike's headquarters are expected to spend a few hours every day in the gym. Knight is not without his detractors, and the biggest criticisms all relate to one of the foundations on which Nike was built: use foreign manufacturing labour to keep costs – and therefore prices – down. Nike has been accused of exploiting poor workers in Asia where the shoes are manufactured. Nike argues that the contractors who supply them are responsible for their workers' pay and conditions, while the critics counter that this is disingenuous and an abdication of responsibility.

Nevertheless, the negative press hasn't prevented Knight from receiving many awards for leadership and management, as if a $6 billion business wasn't evidence enough of his leadership skills. And Nike's focus on innovation and long-term development mean Knight's business is as well placed as any to retain its position as global number one sports shoe company.

22 RAY KROC

1902–1984

Organisation: McDonald's

Key idea: Fast food for the masses

'The definition of salesmanship is the gentle art of letting the customer have it your way.'

R|ay Kroc was, in many ways, one of the most unlikely leaders of a multinational organisation. He was a travelling salesman who was over 50 years old before he launched the McDonald's empire, and 60 by the time he started drawing an income from it. What's more, it wasn't even his own idea. But what Kroc lacked in creativity he made up for in marketing flair and energy, and he knew how to turn this idea he had stumbled across into a winner. Like many great leaders, he never doubted himself or his vision, and he was rewarded for his conviction with the largest restaurant company in the world.

Kroc was a keen pianist, and a career in music had been his first ambition. But it didn't pay the bills so by the age of 20 he was working as a paper cup salesman in the daytime, and playing the piano for a radio station at night. After several years, he encountered a customer for his paper cups who had invented a multimixing machine, which impressed Kroc. His entrepreneurial spirit convinced him to get involved in selling this new machine; he sensed it had great potential. So he acquired the exclusive marketing rights to the machine. He spent the next 17 years travelling the US selling mixers.

Eventually, he found himself dealing with a restaurant in San Bernardino, California, which was owned by two brothers named Dick and Mac McDonald. These two sold a very limited menu of hamburgers, cheeseburgers, fries, milkshakes and soft drinks, but they sold them at very low prices. And what really intrigued Kroc was that the restaurant had invested in eight of his mixers, which seemed to be churning away at full capacity all day.

Ray Kroc ... on leadership

The quality of a leader is reflected in the standards they set for themselves.

Kroc was ready once again to jump on a bandwagon in which he saw potential, and he immediately suggested to the brothers that they open several more restaurants – they could start a chain. To begin with, Kroc saw this as a way to create more customers for his mixers. The McDonalds were unsure about who could open new restaurants for them, but Kroc wasn't. He offered his services, and the brothers accepted.

For the next seven years, Kroc invested everything he had in building up the business, taking no salary except what he was still earning from selling milkshake mixers. It didn't take him long to realise that McDonald's could be far bigger than the mixer business ever was. He said later, 'I was 52 years old. I had diabetes and incipient arthritis. I had lost my gall bladder and most of my thyroid gland in earlier campaigns, but I was convinced that the best was ahead of me.'

He stuck closely to the format the McDonald brothers had devised, of simple fast food at low prices. McDonald's certainly wasn't the first fast food chain, but it was consistently in tune with its public. Kroc was one of those people who could sense what the public wanted, and he realised that people were increasingly eating on the go, going out for food rather than staying in. And speed of service was far more important to them than a relaxed and comfortable dining experience.

Almost the biggest impact Kroc made on the McDonald's style was to put a huge emphasis on cleanliness. From uniforms to equipment, from the car parks to the tables, he believed that to encourage customers McDonald's must have a strong image of being clean, fresh and healthy.

Eventually, in 1961, Kroc persuaded the McDonald brothers (whose confidence was not so strong as his) to sell him the business for $2.7 million. It has since been claimed that he wasn't entirely fair in his dealings with the McDonalds; what is in no dispute is that the sum he paid them turned out to be a bargain price. By 1963, McDonald's had sold a billion hamburgers, and opened its 500th restaurant. Ronald McDonald the clown appeared the same year to promote the chain, and became popular with children across America and beyond.

Ray Kroc never had another big success, despite launching frequent new enterprises with anything between modest success and total

Ray Kroc ... on standards

I emphasise the importance of details. You must perfect every fundamental of your business if you expect it to perform well.

failure. He tried upmarket burger restaurants, pie shops and theme parks. Even his ideas for McDonald's products – the Hula Burger, for example – failed. The best ideas, such as the Big Mac, all came from his franchise operators.

But in a sense this was part of Kroc's strength. Few entrepreneurs are happy to take other people's ideas in preference to their own, but Kroc built his whole business on someone else's idea. And he ran it successfully through his inspired salesmanship, coupled with his skill at spotting talent and recognising good ideas. He took on many key managers who made enormous contributions in fields in which Kroc himself would have floundered, from finance to operational systems.

Another key decision Kroc made in the early days was that he wanted to build an organisation in which everyone would profit from success. So unlike other franchisers at the time, Kroc wanted his operators to be profitable first. This meant selling them supplies and equipment with no mark-up for himself, and it cost McDonald's heavily in the first few years. However, once the operators started to turn healthy profits – and prospective franchisees saw McDonald's as a worthwhile option – Kroc's policy paid substantial dividends.

Ray Kroc remained chairman of McDonald's until his death in 1984. His greatest skills as a leader were his feel for the popular mood, his ability to sell just about any idea to anyone, and his infectious enthusiasm and optimism. These were the qualities that meant it still wasn't too late for a travelling salesman in his fifties to become a billionaire businessman.

EDWIN LAND

1909–1991

Organisation: *Polaroid*

Key idea: *The polaroid camera*

'The only thing that is keeping us alive is our brilliance. The only way to protect our brilliance is patents.'

Edwin Land was a rare type of highly successful business leader for two reasons. For one thing, he wasn't the usual big charismatic personality that typifies the majority of inspirational leaders. And the other unusual factor was that – like Edison – he saw himself as a scientist rather than a businessman.

Edwin Land's fascination with science began when he was a boy. As a small child, he once dismantled the family's phonograph, for which he was soundly spanked by his father. He recalled, 'From then on, I was totally stubborn about being blocked. Nothing or nobody could stop me from carrying through the execution of an experiment.' He used to visit his local library to use the stereopticon, which displayed three-dimensional views of grottoes, and his bedtime reading included textbooks on subjects such as optics.

In 1922, when he was 13, Land went on a summer camp where his teacher showed an experiment which involved using a light-polarising glass crystal to suppress the glare of light from a table top. He was captivated. A few years later he dropped out of Harvard to start experimenting with polarisation. The main application he foresaw was sheets of polarising plastic that could be placed in front of car headlights to get rid of the night time glare.

After a couple of failed attempts, Land came up with an idea that worked. With the help of a loan from his father, he began to develop his invention. He returned to Harvard for three years, where he now had his own lab, and in 1933 finally came up with a product he could patent. Now he quit Harvard again – still without a degree – and set up in partnership with one of his physics tutors, George Wheelwright, to make polarisers for 3-D glasses for watching movies, and for reducing headlight glare. When asked later why Land never finished his Harvard studies, his university friend, the mountaineer and photographer Bradford Washburn, replied, 'He didn't need to.'

Land and Wheelwright called their polarising material polaroid, and did most of their business making sunglasses, and camera filters for Eastman Kodak. They were having trouble selling their new invention to car manufacturers because, although inexpensive in itself, it would require doubling the headlight wattage, which would increase fuel consumption.

Land's contemporaries were hugely impressed by his invention, and he was showered with awards and accolades from the scientific community. Polaroid was described as 'the most significant invention in the field of optics... probably in the last century' by one leading scientist. Wall Street was sufficiently impressed, too, to take the Polaroid Corporation public in 1937, giving Land (still only in his twenties) absolute control for ten years.

Land was starting to worry that it was only a matter of time before car manufacturers – who were still wavering – gave the final thumbs down to his system for reducing glare, and the company could lose a large chunk of its potential market. So he decided to find new applications for polaroid. He was right about the rejection by car manufacturers, but by 1947 he had developed another winning idea. Instant photography. In fact, the spark for this invention had come from his three-year-old daughter when they were on a family holiday. He took a photograph of her, and she then demanded to know why she couldn't see it immediately. Land said, 'Within an hour the camera, the film and the physical chemistry became clear to me.' He first demonstrated his invention to massive press coverage, and by the next year he was ready to launch the new cameras and film.

The corporation didn't have the money for a heavy advertising campaign, so they launched locally in Florida, and relied on word of mouth to develop nationwide sales. They didn't have to wait long. As Land made new advances, the product improved. To begin with the photographs were sepia, but soon they became black-and-white, faster, and less prone to fade. Polaroid cameras became a byword for high technology, and were among the world's most popular cameras. Polaroid Corporation went on to develop film cartridges and a colour-developing process in the 1960s, and by the late 70s it had invented instant film cameras.

Edwin Land ... on the process of innovation

You always start with a fantasy. Part of the fantasy technique is to visualise something as perfect. Then with the experiments you work back from the fantasy to reality, hacking away at the components.

As well as running Polaroid, Land also worked for the US government as an advisor. He worked on the deal to build the U-2 spy plane, and supervised the building of spy satellites. His inventions in the field of 3-D photography were hugely useful to American defence, and his vectography was used to survey the French coast before the Normandy landings. Land finally resigned from his post as presidential advisor after the Watergate scandal, when he was listed as one of Nixon's top '200 enemies'. It was a description of which he was particularly proud since, as he explained, it was an honour he had received without working for it.

It seems strange, on the face of it, that Land should have been such a successful businessman when he was clearly a scientist first and foremost, in his eyes as well as anyone else's. But his father was a businessman, and Land understood many essential business principles better than most scientists. For example, he believed implicitly that all new investments should be funded from retained earnings, not from debt. He was not afraid to be commercial as well as innovative, and had no intellectual snobbery about using his skills to develop products that would appeal to the masses. He insisted that the polaroid camera must retail at just the right price: 'You see you can't make money selling to the very rich; there are too few of them. You can't make money selling to the poor, either.'

Land understood that the only way to stay ahead of the competition was to use every new invention as a stepping-stone to the next. He was constantly pushing to develop new ideas as fast as possible. If he didn't have the ideal lab equipment for an experiment, he insisted that the experiment be done with whatever equipment happened to be available in the building at the time. He was always looking for short cuts, and for ways to use existing knowledge to formulate new ideas. He was hugely creative, and understood the need to fail frequently before you finally succeed. If an experiment didn't work, his favourite next step was to try the opposite. Land received a total of 535 patents, a total surpassed only by Edison.

Edwin Land ... on competition

Work only on problems that are manifestly important and seem to be nearly impossible to solve. That way, you will have a natural market for your product and no competition.

Land always saw the Polaroid Corporation as a research institution, but one that made a profit. He wouldn't allow it to get involved in new developments in an already existing market since he found this boring, and also because the price competition would be too fierce. This would mean shaving profits to the point where they couldn't fund valuable future research. So Land made sure Polaroid only entered markets in which it was alone.

This combination of creativity, financial common sense, a desire for uniqueness and a recognition of the need for popular appeal meant that Land was not only among the foremost scientists of his time, but also among the leading businessmen. He ran Polaroid for nearly fifty years, retiring as CEO in 1980. However he continued to work with the Rowland Foundation, a corporation he had founded in 1960, and made new scientific discoveries about the perception of light and colour. He couldn't stop experimenting, and continued to work until his death.

ESTÉE LAUDER

1908–

Organisation: *Estée Lauder*

Key idea: *Free cosmetics samples*

'If you don't sell, it's not the product that's wrong, it's you.'

E stée Lauder devoted her life to making women beautiful, and launched one of the biggest cosmetics brands ever. The business she started now controls 45 per cent of the US department-store market, and her name stands for quality and elegance. Although Lauder had an eye for what women wanted to buy, that wasn't what made her business so big. She had one great talent that drove her: she was a consummate saleswoman.

Lauder was the daughter of immigrants, whose father ran a hardware store in Queens, New York City. Her father was a Hungarian Jew and her mother a French Roman Catholic; Lauder was determined that she would grow up American. Lauder's uncle was a chemist, and when he began concocting skin creams, Lauder learned from him how to make them herself. In 1930 she married Joseph Lauter, and she began to make and sell her own skin creams.

By 1937, she had started adapting her name from Lauter to Lauder, and her products were beginning to sell. Her marriage, however, was doing less well as she devoted her time to her business. She divorced her husband in 1939, but in 1942 the couple decided to remarry. This time, Joseph gave up his job to help run the company. He looked after the production and finance, while she took charge of sales and marketing.

Lauder was selling her products in beauty shops and resorts, but what she really wanted was to sell them through department stores. And what Lauder wanted, Lauder got. Stanley Marcus, head of Neiman Marcus store in Dallas, once explained: 'It was easier to say yes to Estée than to say no.'

> ## Estée Lauder ... on success
>
> Measure your success in dollars, not degrees.

Not that it was a walkover for Lauder. But she pursued the heads of New York department stores until eventually, in 1948, she was given a counter in Saks Fifth Avenue store. Now she could really start selling. She sent out engraved, personalised invitations to the opening, and personally made up every woman who came to the counter. The queues soon stretched right around the block. Lauder had two key approaches in her sales technique: she gave the customer plenty of personal attention and then – her *coup de grace* – she sent them away with a free sample. It was a genius of an idea; it both generated customer goodwill and brought them back to buy more when the sample ran out.

And Lauder never stopped selling even when the doors closed. She handed out free samples to friends and business associates in the evenings. In 1953, when she launched Youth Dew – the first ever bath oil that was also a perfume – she accidentally on purpose spilled it across the carpet of a department store so that the scent would be broadcast further.

She knew the importance of looking like a professional outfit from the start. When she still employed only one person to answer the phones, her single member of staff had to change her voice to become the accounts department or the packaging department so as to imply a larger organisation. She even signed letters in her maiden name, Mentzer, so customers wouldn't think that only Lauders worked for the company.

Lauder had a very clear image for her 'nice little business' as she called it. She wanted people to associate her products with class and with femininity. Lauder especially liked to give free samples of her cosmetics to people who had a reputation for buying the best, and often handed them out to the celebrities she increasingly entertained to dinner parties. As time went on, she became known for being seen and photographed with the Duchess of Windsor, Princess Diana and the like.

Advertisements for Estée Lauder products always showed the most feminine of women, the image with which her brand has always been associated. But Lauder was always in touch with the times even as she got older, and as the popular image of women changed so did her outlook; she just always stayed at the most feminine end of the contemporary spectrum.

Estée Lauder ... on hard work

I feel every person can have everything if they are willing to work, work, work.

Lauder was a skilled manager and a good judge of the market (although she never led trends), but most of her time was devoted to selling, and it was her brand image and sales technique that made her name. She put huge effort into recruiting and training sales staff who were as impeccably turned out as she was herself, and she would turn up at Saks and other department stores on a Saturday to show the staff how it should be done.

As the business grew, Lauder had the smart idea that she could increase her overall sales if she introduced directly competing brands. So she launched new cosmetics ranges, and bought up other companies, with the result that Estée Lauder now owns or controls numerous brands including Clinique, Aramis, Origins, Prescriptives, Bobbi Brown essentials, Aveda and Donna Karan (although her fellow managers admit that Lauder was never so interested in the brands that didn't carry her name).

In 1960, Lauder went international; her first overseas outlet was at Harrods in London. Lauder never missed an opportunity to sell her products. She travelled the world to be at every opening of every new shop or department store counter, she hosted elegant dinner parties at which she would slip her friends free samples. And her lifestyle mirrored her public image. Even her office in Manhattan looked like an elegant dining room, and she graciously and effortlessly mixed running a business with bringing up a family, many of whom followed her onto the board of the company – her son took over from her as CEO.

When Lauder handed over to her son Leonard Lauder in 1985, two years after her husband's death, he carried on where she left off. Credited as being an excellent strategist, he has kept the business on an upward path – it now turns over more than $3.5 billion a year. But even after retirement Lauder continued to be actively involved, regularly turning up at stores in order to teach the staff how to sell. Her own family still own over 50 per cent of the company's stock, and it is still run true to her principles of a high-class image and the emphasis on face-to-face selling. And nowadays they give away more free samples than ever.

WILLIAM HESKETH LEVER (LORD LEVERHULME)

1851–1925

Organisation: *Lever Brothers (Unilever)*

Key idea: *Selling branded, scented soap*

'Half the money I spend on advertising is wasted. The trouble is, I don't know which half.'

It seems so commonplace now that soap should be pleasantly scented, and stamped with a brand name, that it's hard to imagine what a novel idea it was when William Hesketh Lever first dreamt it up. But this simple idea was the foundation stone of the entire Unilever industry.

Lever lived most of his life in the Victorian age. Born in Bolton, Lancashire, in 1851 he worked in his father's wholesale grocery business with his brother, James D'Arcy Lever. The industrialisation of Britain in the second half of the 19th century meant that industries like theirs had millions of new customers, as working-class families began to have enough money to spend on household essentials. Products began to be packaged and branded in order to sell them to this new market.

One of the products Lever sold in his father's store was soap. This was manufactured in long bars which were sliced up by the grocer to each customer's order. It was fairly unpleasant smelling, took a long time to dissolve, and gave relatively little lather. It occurred to Lever that he could do better than this.

So he developed a new recipe for soap which would be softer – so it dissolved faster and lathered better – and would smell sweet. Not only did he devise a better product, he packaged it individually and branded it by imprinting the brand name directly on to the soap: *Sunlight*. With product development and packaging sorted out, Lever turned to marketing, and immediately launched a high-profile advertising campaign for his soap: 'Why does a woman look old sooner than a man? Because she doesn't use *Sunlight*.'

Lever's soap was launched in 1885, and the mass advertising was a huge success, making *Sunlight* one of the first nationally recognised brand names. As Thomas J. Barratt, who ran the Pears soap company, once remarked: 'Any fool can make soap. It takes a clever man to sell it.' Lever and his brother set up their own company, Lever Brothers, to manufacture and sell their soaps.

As well as being a talented businessman, Lever was also an idealist. He supported the Liberal party, which championed industry, democratic reform and free trade. He believed in the principle that the foundation of morality lies in the creation of the greatest possible happiness for the greatest possible number of people. So he determined that his new business should be used to the good of society. By 1887 the company was doing so well that they had to invest in a new manufacturing plant. So Lever and his brother began to build a new factory on the Wirral peninsula. By the time it was completed in 1889 it was the biggest soap works in the world.

Lever surrounded his new factory with a purpose built town to house the workers. In pursuit of his social ideals, he created the most pleasant town he could. The 890 houses were bordered by gardens, and were designed in various styles, even including reproductions of Ann Hathaway's cottage in Stratford-upon-Avon. The town was named after the soap, Port Sunlight. The new town had its own church, school, hotel, gymnasium, theatre, village halls, library, training centre and an open-air swimming pool. After his wife's death Lever even added an art gallery, named after her.

Although Lever believed he was creating the perfect town for his workers, not all of them agreed entirely. Lever was something of a puritan, and in exchange for living under his patronage, workers were not permitted to gamble or even to drink alcohol. Lever was confident that he knew best for his employees, and introduced a 'prosperity-sharing' scheme under which it was he who decided how money should be spent at Port Sunlight. He told his employees that if he gave them an end of year bonus they would be wasting it if they spent it on whisky or the Christmas goose. So he would keep it himself, and spend it on 'everything which makes life pleasant – nice houses, comfortable homes, and healthy recreation.' Despite his good intentions, one of Lever's trade union officials complained to him that 'no man of an independent turn of mind can breathe for long in the atmosphere of Port Sunlight.'

Lever had political aspirations, too, and stood unsuccessfully for parliament three times in Birkenhead in the 1890s. But in 1900 he moved to the Wirral constituency – traditionally a Tory stronghold – and won the seat thanks to the Conservatives' catastrophic policy of increasing duties on imported goods. In 1910, however, he moved to Ormskirk and lost, as did his successor at the Wirral which turned Tory once again.

It wasn't long before Lever expanded his operation overseas, despite the Liberal party's anti-imperialist stance. By the turn of the century he had factories in Australia, New Zealand, South Africa and the United States. Lever's original recipe for soap had relied on using vegetable oils instead of tallow to make the soap soft, and now he decided to buy up plantations to ensure his own supply of raw materials. So in 1905 he bought 50,000 acres in the Solomon Isles in order to plant coconut seed. He expanded this initial land purchase, and added other plantations in the Belgian Congo and West Africa. His operations were boosted during World War I when German vegetable oil supplies from West Africa were cut off, and many of them were diverted to Lever Brothers.

Over time, Lever gradually expanded Lever Brothers. He turned out to be a skilled deal-maker, and bought up most of his competitors in Britain, Australia and South Africa, eventually acquiring his old rival, Pears soap. He began to market Lifebuoy soap, and Lux soap flakes with his usual enthusiasm for mass advertising. During the war, Lever also found a useful outlet for one of the by-products of soap making: glycerine. He delivered this to British arms manufacturers to help them make explosives. It was this contribution to the war effort that earned him his life peerage. Lever took the title Lord Leverhulme, a combination of his own name and his wife's maiden name.

Lever also branched into another new industry during World War I: margarine production. The government was worried that the country was over-dependent on foreign sources for its edible fats – an important staple. So it asked Lever Brothers to make margarine – invented nearly fifty years earlier. The company was an obvious choice since soap and margarine both rely on the same basic raw ingredient: vegetable fat. Margarine turned out to be a key part of Lever Brothers' enduring success as a business.

Leverhulme had plenty of business interests outside Lever Brothers, including buying up the Hebridean islands of Harris and Lewis. Here he set up a whole raft of related industries – trawlers, canneries,

William Hesketh Lever ... on his vision for Port Sunlight

It is my hope, and my brother's hope, to build houses in which our work-people will be able to live and be comfortable. Semi-detached houses, with gardens back and front, in which they will be able to know more about the science of life than they can in a back slum, and in which they will learn that there is more enjoyment in life than in mere going to and returning from work, and looking forward to Saturday night to draw their wages.

and a chain of fish-and-chip shops called Mac Fisheries. In order to supply this chain with meat products, he also acquired a sausage manufacturer named Thomas Walls. This business turned out to have a seasonal slump in the summer, so it began to manufacture ice cream to fill in the slack period. Eventually, Lord Leverhulme was forced to give up his development of the Western Isles because of local opposition – he was accused of trying to 'create for himself a feudal estate'. In 1922 he sold off all his private business enterprises, including Mac Fisheries and Walls, to his own business, Lever Brothers.

Lord Leverhulme died in 1925, four years before the massive merger with the Margarine Union which created Unilever on 1 January 1930. The organisation continued to build on Leverhulme's principles of frequent acquisitions and mass advertising of consumer products. It now owns brands around the world, from Brooke Bond and Bird's Eye to Vaseline and Oxo, and is the world's largest consumer products company, employing 350,000 people.

SPEDAN LEWIS

1885–1963

Organisation: *John Lewis Partnership*

Key idea: *Profit sharing*

'There may be people who will devote themselves to the invention of a new system of business for its own sake, exactly as a man may devote himself to scientific research.'

S pedan Lewis was an extraordinary man by any standards. He had a vision of a completely new way of organising a business, and he had the opportunity to put his ideas to the test. It was a remarkable vision not least because it required considerable financial sacrifice on his part, and even a harsh reduction in his own power as a leader. But he stuck to his vision regardless. He was disappointed that other businesses didn't follow his lead but the success of his own organisation, the John Lewis Partnership, is a testament to the validity and feasibility of his plan.

Speedan Lewis was the elder son of John Lewis, a draper from Shepton Mallet in the West Country who had moved to London and set up shop in Oxford Street. He was successful enough to send his son to Westminster School. When Spedan Lewis was 19, he went into his father's business and, two years later, his father gave him £50,000 capital and a 25 per cent share in the shop. His father, meanwhile, was buying an ailing shop in Sloane Square named Peter Jones, and he soon gave Spedan a seat on the board there.

Spedan Lewis was troubled in his work, however. He was becoming increasingly conscious of the wide disparity between the money his father made from the business, and that made by the employees. His father had accrued so much wealth that he could only spend a fraction of it, yet most of the staff could only dream of having enough money to save anything at all.

Lewis later explained, 'My father's success had been due to his try-ing constantly to give very good value to people who wished to exchange their money for his merchandise. But it also became clear to me that the business would have grown further ... if he had done the same for those who wished to exchange their work for his money.'

Lewis wanted to come up with a way of sharing profits with em-ployees, which involved distributing what had until now been reserves, but he couldn't see a way to expand the business if all the profits were given out. Then it dawned on him that a limited liability company could finance its own growth and share profits in the form of shares rather than cash. Some profit could be capitalised each year, and so long as the shares were non-voting, employees could choose whether to sell or retain them without affecting the control of the business.

Lewis' father, however, was not impressed. He could see that this would mean a far smaller remuneration for the owner, and asked his son whom he thought would run the business 'for such a miserable re-muneration as this would mean?' Lewis could not see a way to put his ideas into practice, at least not while his father had control of the busi-ness.

In 1914, when Lewis was 29, his father gave him managerial control of Peter Jones. At last he could try out some of his ideas, although his father still held the majority of the shares. Lewis began by improving conditions. He shortened the working day by an hour, and set up a sys-tem of staff committees at which elected representatives of the rank and file staff – without their managers – met with the chairman and dis-cussed any issues they wanted to raise with him. Lewis also instituted a system of commission, pooled in each department, to help incentivise the sales staff. He raised salaries across the board, too, and kept two sets of books: the real ones, and a set for his father to look at which didn't show the salary increases.

Within a couple of years, Lewis had fallen out with his father over the John Lewis store and they agreed to operate more independently of each other. Spedan Lewis exchanged his 25 per cent share in the John Lewis shop for his father's controlling share in Peter Jones. At last he had his own business to do as he liked with.

One of the first things Lewis did was to start recruiting exception-ally well-educated people to senior management posts. He continued to improve conditions by giving employees a third week's paid holiday a year (unheard of in the retail trade). He launched an internal weekly newspaper, *The Gazette*, in which he invited any staff to write in, anony-mously if they wished, and have their letters published. It was also a means for all members of the company to keep in touch with news and

---

Spedan Lewis ... on the employer/employee relationship

The relation of employers to employees should be that of lawyers or stockbrokers to their clients, or of doctors to their patients, or of teachers and trainers to their students. None of these experts ask for their services more than a definite fee quite moderate in relation to the importance of the service they give for it. Beyond that fixed amount the whole of the benefit goes to the client or patient or pupil.

---

ideas. Lewis also set up a representative staff council. And by 1920, the first formal profit-making scheme was launched, and Lewis introduced the practice of referring to employees as 'partners'.

Although trade was improving a little, Lewis needed to raise cash to invest in further growth, so he was obliged to sell his own home and move into a flat in London. But the national slump hit the store hard, and profits disappeared until Peter Jones was finally bailed out by Lewis' father a few years later. From then on, the store began to thrive under the new system, and by 1925 profits were good and staff were paid 'partnership benefit' equivalent to seven weeks' pay.

In 1926, Lewis' younger brother Oswald relinquished his 25 per cent share in the John Lewis shop to Spedan and, with his father aged 90 and ailing, Spedan Lewis was now effectively the manager of both Peter Jones and John Lewis. On his father's death two years later he inherited full control. Lewis immediately made sure that his ideas of partnership were applied to the whole of his newly expanded enterprise, and in 1929 he formally transferred his interest in the company to a Trust on behalf of everyone who worked in it.

Lewis continued to run the business he had transformed until his retirement in 1955, since when the partnership has remained successfully in place. The business continued to grow massively, buying up other stores and the Waitrose chain of supermarkets. Although the partnership arrangement certainly helped to motivate the staff, Lewis was also a talented manager in other ways. He introduced the famous slogan 'never knowingly undersold', and he had an instinct for buying and selling.

Lewis did much of the buying for John Lewis, and often found new lines that were a big success. According to his successor, Sir Bernard Miler, 'On other occasions he bought things, marked them very cheaply, but they didn't sell. He would then say: 'We probably marked them too cheaply', upped the price and sold the lot. He had that sort of flair for

---

Spedan Lewis ... on salaries

You can't sleep in more than one bed at a time, and once you've got three motor cars what do you want any more for?

---

retailing.' Lewis also had a flair for stock control and organisational management, and he was a very skilled interviewer, selecting and appointing talented managers to work under him.

Despite his concern for his employees, or partners, and his great kindness at times, he was also an unexpectedly difficult and cantankerous man. He would fire people on the spot on quite flimsy grounds, and sometimes even re-employ them later. One of his personal assistants, Jack Webster, was recruited to the management team. After about a year, Lewis said to him, over a game of golf, 'I think you ought to go back to the job you came from.' Webster replied, 'I can't do that, because it isn't there.' About half an hour later, Lewis suddenly said, 'Would you like to be my personal assistant?' Webster started next morning, and stayed in the job for seven years.

Lewis retired at the age of 70, having effectively written himself out of the job. For the next eight years until his death he griped regularly at the way the business was being run, and was angry and upset that no one asked his advice any more. What he failed to appreciate was that his successors were simply following his own design, and practising what he had preached – they were putting the Partnership first.

WILLIAM LYONS
1901–1985

Organisation: *Jaguar*

Key idea: *Affordable style*

'Motoring should be a joy and not a chore.'

Many of the most famous cars were named after their makers: Porsche, Ferrari, Ford. But not Jaguar. The man behind the company never earned the fame outside the industry that many of his fellow makers did, but William Lyons created in Jaguar one of the most famous cars ever, and a company that still follows his principles over a decade after his death. Although Jaguars were never the cheapest cars on the market, they were always outstanding value for money, and the name Jaguar is synonymous with style and understated elegance.

Lyons was the son of an Irish music shop owner, and grew up in Blackpool at the beginning of the 20th century. He grew up with a passion for motorbikes. It so happened that just across the road from his parents house lived a family called the Walmsleys, whose son William was ten years older than Lyons, and had a small business making motorbike sidecars in his parents' garage. He made an unusual octagonal sidecar named the Swallow, and young Lyons bought one from him for his Norton motorbike.

Lyons was attracted to the stylishness of this sidecar, and reckoned other people would be too. So he suggested that Walmsley and he go into business together. Despite being only 20 years old, he was sufficiently convincing with his ideas for improving production that he persuaded Walmsley to take him on as a partner. One of Lyons' great attributes was his business sense, and he began by talking Walmsley into taking on a larger workspace.

With financial help from both sets of parents, the two men formed the Swallow Sidecar Company in 1922. The stylish sidecars did indeed sell well, just as Lyons had predicted, and before long the company was making its own cars, too. The emphasis was on style – they used the Austin engine and chassis – and they produced an elegant two-seater car. They even finished their cars in two-tone colours, at a time when almost all cars were black.

By 1928, Lyons and Walmsley decided to move to Coventry, which had become the centre of the British car building industry. Lyons constantly came up with new and better production methods, and production increased to 50 cars a week. Swallow cars had a sense of style ahead of their time, thanks to Lyons. He wasn't an engineer, but he knew what looked good, and for nearly 50 years he made sure none of his cars were ever made without his input into the design. Even back in the 1920s his cars had the low-profile characteristic of all his cars.

In 1931, Lyons decided that working with another manufacturer's engine and chassis was too restrictive, so he and Walmsley designed their own chassis and had it custom built to their specification, to match a standard engine. This new car was called the SS1 (there was also a smaller model, the SS2), and was an instant hit for its striking appearance. It was described at the time by *The Motor* magazine as 'a car built for the connoisseur but relatively low priced.' It was a prediction of the direction Swallow and Jaguar would take in the future.

There was much speculation – and sometimes still is – over what the initials SS stood for. But as with Heinz's '57 varieties' (a number plucked from the air), there wasn't an answer to the question. Lyons was passionate about Brough Superior motorbikes, which used the designation SS, and this may have influenced him. He later said, 'There was much speculation as to whether SS stood for Standard Swallow or Swallow Special – it was never resolved.'

Walmsley was happy to watch his company doing comfortable business with the SS1 and 2, but Lyons thought they could do even better with a higher performance engine. So he decided to develop a new engine. Walmsley wasn't keen to keep up with the pace, so he and Lyons separated amicably, Lyons buying out Walmsley, and Lyons then took the company public in 1934.

Lyons was not only a skilled business operator, he also knew his own limitations. So he hired the best engineers he could find, knowing that his strengths lay in styling and in running the business. Lyons told his engineers he wanted a car with performance to match its looks. He unveiled his new car, the Jaguar, to an impressed audience of dealers who collectively estimated the cost of the car at about double the actual selling price. Lyons had once again created a car at a price that was a fraction of what it seemed to be worth.

William Lyons ... on Jaguar design

The only space in some of our Jaguars is the boot.

The company continued to grow through the thirties, although the war interrupted production as Lyons' company manufactured key aircraft components, sidecars and jeep-type vehicles. Lyons made sure his best engineers always did fire-watch duty together, so they could discuss ideas ready for when the company returned to business. After the war, the initials SS no longer seemed like a good name to use, so Lyons renamed his company Jaguar Cars Ltd. Production resumed, and now Lyons began to export his cars too, especially to North America.

Lyons' dream now was to build a luxury saloon that could reach 100 mph. He launched a series of successful cars, each coming a little closer than before to this golden milestone Lyons had set himself. At last, in 1948, Lyons' engineers came up with an engine that could reach 120 mph. Lyons called his new car the XK120, and launched it at the Motor Show. Only 200 were going to be made, but the car was such a success that production had to be expanded fast.

By the 1950s and 1960s, Jaguar was established as one of the leading car manufacturers in the world. Lyons took Jaguar into motor racing, which was an excellent form of cheap advertising at the time. Once Lyons was sure his cars wouldn't 'embarrass themselves' he quickly established them in the top class of racing cars. In 1956, the Queen visited the Jaguar factory in Coventry and knighted Lyons.

Lyons was always the driving force behind Jaguar's design, and often the answer to questions about the reasoning behind aspects of Jaguar's styling was simply 'That's how Lyons wanted it.' On one occasion, Lyons was at a New York motor show when an XK140 owner complained to him that his heater didn't work. Lyons went to his car and declared, 'The heater does work.' He got the customer to turn on the engine, and held a cigarette in front of the heater. The smoke was blown gently away, and Lyons remarked, 'Look, it works perfectly.' His customer protested explaining, 'But temperatures get to 15 below zero.' Lyons replied: 'Young man, you just put on an overcoat.'

In 1966, Lyons decided to ensure Jaguar's survival by merging his company into the British Motor Corporation, which formed into British Leyland two years later. It nearly spelt the end for Jaguar which was threatened with losing its identity, but unlike many other companies such as MG and Austin, Lyons had insisted Jaguar remain an individual business entity.

By now, Lyons was well into his 60s. But he was determined to create one more masterpiece before he retired. In 1968 he launched it: the XJ6, still regarded as a style classic. It had all the trademarks of Lyons' unique styling, a sleek, low sports saloon with first class performance. It was his own favourite car.

In 1972, Lyons finally retired, 50 years after he founded the company. His superb business acumen, coupled with hiring the best people, and rounded off with his own superb eye for styling, had created a legend of a car business. He died in 1985, and Jaguar style has never been quite the same without him. But his legacy remains strong in the business, and individual style and character is still the Jaguar trademark, thanks to Lyons.

BERNARD MARCUS

1929–

Organisation: *Home Depot*

Key idea: *The warehouse DIY store*

'I never had anybody work for me in retailing who didn't work for me out of love, as opposed to fear. We care about each other and we care about the customer.'

ernard Marcus came from nowhere and then got fired. But he still went on to build the world's biggest home improvement retail chain, with his partner Arthur Blank, and to turn the industry upside down. His company's finest hour was when it was added to the Dow Jones Industrial Average ousting its competitor Sears, along with others such as Chevron and Goodyear.

Marcus grew up in a tenement in Newark, New Jersey, the son of Russian immigrants. Marcus decided while he was still at school that he wanted to become a doctor – he was a big fan of Freud and even learnt to use hypnosis – so he decided to work to pay his way through college. He took a series of jobs, from waiter to MC, and enrolled at Rutgers University. But money was still tight, so he had to transfer to the pharmacy school and graduated in 1952 as a pharmacist instead of a doctor.

Beginning with jobs in a drugstore and a cosmetics company, Marcus found his way into retailing. He gradually worked his way through several companies, ending up as a senior executive at Handy Dan Home Improvement Centers. While he was there, he encountered another executive named Arthur Blank, whom he recruited to the executive team. Both men clashed several times with their boss, and after a corporate buyout in 1978 they were both fired.

By now Marcus was 49, and the logical next move was to take another senior management job somewhere. But instead, Marcus and Blank decided to use their experience in the home improvement retail industry and set up their own business. They figured they could do it better than anyone else. So in 1979 they opened their first three stores, in Atlanta, Georgia. Their stores were big, with a huge number of lines and cheap prices. They grossed $7 million but still lost $1 million. But in 1980, the stores went into profit, and in 1981 Home Depot went public, raising $4 million.

This influx of cash enabled Marcus and Blank to open more stores in neighbouring states, pushing sales into the tens of millions. Growth never stopped, and by 1999 net sales were $38.4 billion. Home Depot has hundreds of stores across the US, Canada and South America, and employs nearly a quarter of a million people.

So what was the secret? What did Marcus and his partner do that no one else was doing? They created a new concept in home improvement stores, built on three principles: first, the wide-open warehouse store that sold to amateur DIYers as well as the traditional customer base of professional contractors. Each Home Depot store carries between 40,000 and 50,000 lines.

Second, this massive inventory allowed Home Depot to offer ludicrously low prices, often undercutting the competition by as much as 40 per cent. Marcus always adopted a policy of selling good-quality merchandise; it's cheap because Home Depot's costs are low, not because it's rubbish. And it's also cheap because that's the policy. The idea is not to charge as much as the company can get away with, but to make low prices integral to the brand. Marcus learnt a great deal from Sam Walton at Wal-Mart about pricing low for its own sake.

And third, Marcus and Blank's other great innovation from the start was to put the emphasis firmly on customer service. By 1980, the year after the first stores opened, Home Depot had instituted a programme of regular product knowledge training sessions, to make sure that sales assistants really knew their products. This training is still a cornerstone of the Home Depot ethos. Blank actually spends a third of his time training staff – unheard of for a CEO.

As well as detailed knowledge of the lines they sell, staff also offer first rate personal service. Marcus says, 'If ever I saw an associate [as they term their employees] point a customer toward what they needed three aisles over, I would threaten to bite their finger. I would say, "Don't ever let me see you point. You take the customer by the hand, and you bring them right where they need to be and you help them."' In the early 1980s, Marcus' chief worry about Home Depot's ability to grow fast was the problem of recruiting and training new staff to such high standards in a short time.

Marcus has always adopted a hands-on management policy, and spends a great deal of time in the stores. Often he turns up unan-

Bernard Marcus ... on shareholding employees

They own a 'piece of the rock', and this is their piece of America.

nounced. As one Home Depot executive has explained, 'Bernie will go up to the tool area as if he knows nothing about the business and say, "Tell me what your bestselling hammer is." If it isn't obvious from the display, then we're not giving the customer what they want.'

The customers, in fact, clearly know exactly what they want, and Marcus and his partner don't hesitate to ask them. As a result Home Depot offers services such as free design and decorating consultations, tool rental, home delivery, free potting and the like. In fact, 70 per cent of Home Depot's 50,000 lines have been suggested by customers.

Marcus and Blank adopted a policy of looking after their employees and giving them responsibility from the start. They have always paid the best wages in the industry, with generous stock-purchase plans, and the excellent training they give also helps to inspire a high level of loyalty among their associates.

Responsibility is also devolved as far as possible. Marcus and Blank created a strategy of giving each store as local a feel as possible, and they have decentralised decision making as far as possible to achieve this. They have a highly effective management structure whereby store managers report to a regional manager through whom they can access all the organisation's functional departments: legal, advertising, information services, merchandise accounting and so on. Senior management also has direct links to individual stores via their own television network so that it can get feedback direct from local managers, and can watch training programmes in progress. Marcus likes to keep a relaxed corporate culture in which every manager feels able to report to anyone. The decentralised decision-making system means that individual store managers can adapt advertising or product displays, and change the order for a product, so long as they can justify their decision.

Decentralisation also means that local managers have the authority to help their local community. Philanthropy is an important part of the Home Depot culture; the 2000 budget was over $25 million. This money is directed at the local communities around the stores, and managers are encouraged to contribute time and leadership to local projects as well as money.

Home Depot's management is the envy of the industry, and has helped it become the second biggest retailer in the world, behind Wal-

Bernard Marcus ... on philanthropy

When the Home Depot went public, we realised that we had the financial capacity and wherewithal to give back to the communities where we did business. There is a concept in Judaism called tzedaka, which means 'to give back'. It is considered a mitzvah, a good deed, to give to someone who doesn't have, and we believe strongly in giving back to the community.

Mart. One Wal-Mart executive has even gone so far as to say, 'Home Depot is the best-managed retail company in America, ours included.'

SIMON MARKS (LORD MARKS)

1888–1964

Organisation: *Marks & Spencer*

Key idea: *Consumers will pay more for better quality*

'I am the greatest rebel of you all.'

Although Simon Marks did not actually start his own business, he transformed his father's penny bazaars out of all recognition, and built a modestly successful chain of stores into a multinational corporation. His great innovation was to turn on its head the traditional system of retailing – in which retailers bought what the manufacturer offered – and instead to dictate to the manufacturers what he wanted them to supply. Like so many inspired ideas it has become so widely practised that it now seems obvious.

Simon Marks' company had been built up from nothing by his father, Michael Marks, who had fled to England at the age of 19 as a refugee from Poland, escaping a wave of pogroms. Unable to speak a word of English, he had persuaded a stranger he met (who spoke a little Yiddish) to lend him £5 to set himself up as a peddler. Since he couldn't converse with his customers, he pinned a notice on the front of his tray which read, 'Don't ask the price, it's a penny.'

This concept was so successful that Michael Marks soon had a stall in Leeds Market called Marks Penny Bazaar. Soon, other traders were trying to set up nearby to benefit from the increased traffic around Marks' stall. Before long, Marks had opened his penny bazaars in other towns in the north-east. The work of running this business was expanding, so Marks took on a partner recommended by his original benefactor. His new partner was called Thomas Spencer, and they called their company Marks & Spencer. By the time Michael Marks died in 1907 – aged only 44 – the business had 49 shops and market stalls and a turnover of £169,000.

Thomas Spencer had died two years earlier, so now his executor took over the company, since young Simon Marks was still only 19. But Marks was ambitious and after four years he had managed to win himself a seat on the board. Eventually, in 1916, he took over as chairman of Marks & Spencer and finally had control of his father's company.

Marks recognised that things were changing, and it was only a matter of time before his business would either fail or be taken over. For one thing, the one-penny price ceiling was becoming unrealistic with wartime shortages and raw materials prices on the rise. And then there was the competition. F W Woolworth had arrived from America in 1909 with its big, light and airy 'threepence and sixpence' stores (equivalent to the US 'five and dime'), and their higher price ceiling was low enough to appeal and yet high enough to give greater variety and quality than Marks could. Marks knew he had to do something.

One of the first things he did was to visit America, and find out how their chain stores operated. What he saw led him to make three important changes when he returned. The first was to open more spacious stores, where he could show off his goods better. Next was the introduction of new accounting machines, which gave him a system of stock and sales control so advanced that it wasn't replaced until the mid-1980s. And the third big change was a new price ceiling of five shillings, jumping Marks & Spencer up to a premium market position ahead of Woolworth. Marks & Spencer went public in 1926 to fund the expansion that was needed for the new stores.

But Marks still had a problem: the five-shilling price ceiling. He was starting to realise that as standards of living increased his customers were looking for quality, not just low prices. He could see that he had to offer good value, but that didn't have to mean the lowest prices. So how could he provide really good quality at prices that were still affordable?

The answer was to decide what he wanted to sell and then specify it to the manufacturer. It wasn't the way things were done – retailers had always said yea or nay to the goods on offer – but Marks could see it was the way things would have to be done in future. There could be no more buying from wholesalers; he would have to go direct to the makers.

But it wasn't easy. By now, Marks had persuaded his old school friend and brother-in-law Israel Sieff to join him as vice-chairman, and it was his task to get the manufacturers to deal directly with them. But they didn't want to. For a start, the wholesalers had a powerful hold over the manufacturers and threatened to blacklist any who sold direct to retailers. And also, Marks & Spencer still had a 'bottom end of the market' image, which deterred many manufacturers too. Israel Sieff was having problems.

Simon Marks ... on priorities

I set out to build a business, not a fortune.

Sieff had already tried to do business with a textile manufacturer called Corah, but had been politely refused. Undeterred, he tried again, and was dismissed once more. But Corah's production director, Cecil Coleman, escorted him to the door, taking him through the men's sock department on the way. Sieff pointed out to Coleman that many of his machines were standing idle, but that he could give him an order for five hundred dozen socks a week in three colours. Coleman, astounded, responded that if Sieff placed an order on the spot, he'd do business with him.

Coleman didn't dare tell his bosses, Jack and Reggie Corah, that he was supplying Marks & Spencer, so he supplied them secretly under a code name. But eventually a package for Marks & Spencer was misdirected to another customer, and the Corahs found out. They sacked Coleman on the spot. They then investigated just how much business Coleman had been doing with Sieff, and discovered it accounted for over 50 per cent of their business. So Coleman was reinstated.

Although the Corahs continued to keep the arrangement secret, eventually it became known; it turned out to be the breakthrough Marks had needed, as more manufacturers agreed to do business with his company. But many were still reluctant to use their own trademarks on the goods, so Marks devised his own. Corah's trademark was 'St Margaret', and Marks copied this using his father's name instead: St Michael.

Marks had realised his aim of raising value by dealing direct with manufacturers, but his desire to create better quality at affordable prices didn't stop there. He knew that to get the best from their suppliers, he and Sieff would have to find ways of harnessing new technology and innovation to give them better quality at a reduced cost. Marks lived in a London square where he often used to go for walks. One day he happened to meet an inventor and businessman in the square named Henry Dreyfus. Dreyfus was trying to develop commercial markets for his new cellulose acetate and Marks asked if he could make material to Marks & Spencer's specification, and deliver it direct to their manufacturers. The result was a new rayon which became the material for Marks & Spencer's ladies' underwear.

In time, Marks set up a textile laboratory in his Baker Street headquarters to assess new materials for use in Marks & Spencer's clothing.

Simon Marks ... on specialising

You either make things or you sell them. Don't try both!

After World War II, Marks sensed that women would want light, bright clothes to wear after the drab clothing of the war years, so he added a design department under a top designer.

Marks, and his vice-chairman Sieff, had created a revolution in retailing. To this day, Marks & Spencer still sell only products that have been specified exclusively by them. They determine the raw materials and the production methods so they control the entire supply chain. It was Marks solution to the basic question of how to ensure maximum quality at minimum cost.

KONOSUKE MATSUSHITA

1894–1989

Organisation: *Matsushita Electric*

Key idea: *Customer service*

'We are going to win and the industrial West is going to lose out; there's not much you can do about it because the reasons for your failure are within yourselves.'

During the world exposition in Osaka in 1970, over 7.5 million people visited the Matsushita pavilion. One day the manager in charge of the stand was looking at the CCTV screens when he saw Konosuke Matsushita himself queueing patiently to get in. He rushed out to welcome him, and asked 'Why are you standing here in line?' Matsushita replied, 'Oh, I just thought I'd find out how much time people had to wait before they could get in.' It was typical of the man who famously never lost touch with the front line of his business.

Matsushita was born in a small village in Japan in 1894. By the age of nine he was orphaned and began working, first in a bicycle shop and then at the Osaka Electric Light Company. At the age of 23 he opened his own shop, selling a new electric light socket he had designed. He had three employees and almost no capital. In fact, the socket was not a success, but his next invention was: an electric plug which was cheap enough to make that he could undercut the competition by 30 per cent. Within a year, Matsushita Electric was employing 20 people.

In 1923, Matsushita came up with a new invention: a battery-powered bicycle lamp. Until then, bicycle lamps were candle or oil fuelled, and a lamp that would run independently for up to 40 hours was a breakthrough. Matsushita sold his new invention directly to retailers; his usual sales technique was to visit them with one of his bicycle lamps, turn it on and then leave, saying 'If you're impressed, you know where to find me.'

Now things were really starting to take off; and Matsushita Electric began to build a network of sales agents across Japan. One of Matsushita's great heroes was Henry Ford, and he adopted Ford's approach of attracting a mass market by forcing down prices so as to drive up sales. By 1932, Matsushita had taken out 280 patents and had over 1000 employees.

Despite his talent as an inventor, however, it is as a business entrepreneur and leader that he is justly most lauded. He largely left the product development to his R&D department, while he concentrated on marketing and customer service. Matsushita began advertising his products in newspapers as early as 1927 – an almost unheard of move at the time.

During the economic slump of the late 1920s, Matsushita Electric continued to grow, thanks to its founder's management methods. For a start, Matsushita placed enormous emphasis on customer service: 'After-sales service is more important than assistance before sales. It is through such service that one gets permanent customers.' This, combined with the company's low price strategy and huge efficiency in areas such as stock control, ensured that Matsushita's customers stayed loyal.

Matsushita continued to emphasise the importance of customer service as his organisation grew, and he insisted on keeping in touch with his customers. Whenever he visited the retailers who sold his products, he would talk not only to the shop manager, but to every sales assistant, asking how customers viewed his products.

When the recession deepened in 1930, Matsushita didn't want to fire his factory workers. So instead he turned them all into salesmen and sent them out to sell the backlog of unsold stock. During the war, Matsushita turned his factories over to the war effort and made ships and planes – despite having no previous experience of either. Following the war, he was instrumental in rebuilding the Japanese economy, and was responsible for giving Japanese householders 'three treasures': a washing machine, refrigerator and television at prices they could afford.

The organisation went from strength to strength, and Matsushita created the world famous brand Panasonic on his way to building a business with revenue of well over $40 billion, as well as amassing a personal fortune of $3 billion.

Matsushita was a true entrepreneur who believed that all business people should aim 'to make all products as inexhaustible and as cheap as tap water'. In 1931 he bought an expensive patent vital for making radios, and then made it available free to all competing manufacturers

> ### Konosuke Matsushita ... on responsibilities at the top
>
> Big things and little things are my job. Middle-level arrangements can be delegated.

in order to stimulate growth. He developed VHS video at around the same time that Sony developed Betamax. Unlike Sony, however, Matsushita licensed the VHS technology. Despite the fact that Betamax was undoubtedly superior to VHS, it was Matsushita's technology that became the standard.

Matsushita developed an innovative management style as his business grew. While Western companies were centralising power, Matsushita split his organisation into divisions to devolve as much power as possible. He wanted to cultivate a spirit of entrepreneurism in each employee, giving them a sense of direct responsibility: 'It's not enough to work conscientiously. No matter what kind of job, you should think of yourself as being completely in charge of and responsible for your own work.'

Matsushita once asked one of his section chiefs whether all his team leaders obeyed his instructions. When he replied that they did, Matsushita replied: 'You're very lucky. You know, people think I'm a dictatorial businessman. But actually, only about 40 percent of the decisions I approve are ones I really agree with. The others I have reservations about, but you can't say no to everything. Issuing orders directly to get things done the way you want them done is one way of operating, but I think a person in charge of others has to OK some things he doesn't really like. Then, in the process of implementation, you work to guide them along the path you think best.'

Matsushita was a father figure to his employees, admired for his concern for them – both materially and spiritually – as well as for his business acumen. This spiritual aspect of the man also guided his business practices. He believed that profit alone was not sufficient motive for running a business. He declared, 'The mission of a manufacturer should be to overcome poverty, to relieve society as a whole from misery, and bring it wealth.' In 1946, following the war, Matsushita founded the PHP (Peace, Happiness, Prosperity) Institute, a think tank with the aim of bringing peace, happiness and prosperity to the world.

Matsushita's beliefs are enshrined in his company's management objectives: 'Recognising our responsibilities as industrialists, we will devote ourselves to the progress and development of society and the

---

Konosuke Matsushita ... on leadership

The tail trails the head. If the head moves fast, the tail will keep up the same pace. If the head is sluggish, the tail will droop.

---

well-being of people through our business activities, thereby enhancing the quality of life throughout the world.'

Perhaps Matsushita's greatest talent as a leader was his ability to develop and adapt. He started as a gifted inventor, became an entrepreneur when he needed to, adapted to become a successful businessman, and then learnt to manage a huge corporation and become an inspirational leader – a philosopher – to his employees. Throughout his career he continued to exercise the entrepreneur's skill for risk taking, coupled with his unshakeable focus on the customer. As he used to preach to his employees: 'Never forget that every single person you meet is a customer.'

CHARLES MERRILL

1885–1956

Organisation: *Merrill Lynch*

Key idea: *Bringing Wall Street to Main Street*

'America's industrial machine is owned at the grass roots, where it should be, and not in some mythical Wall Street.'

B efore Charles Merrill, Wall Street was effectively run by insiders, and ordinary citizens didn't get a look in. To Merrill, this was all wrong. He believed that all Americans should have the opportunity to invest in America's economy, and he gave them that opportunity. Sure, he wasn't averse to making a bob or two out of them in the process, but he was a real visionary who predicted many trends and events – including the Great Wall Street Crash of 1929.

Merrill didn't have a particularly auspicious start in life. He came from a Florida backwater, the son of a rural doctor and pharmacist. He went to college in Massachusetts where he had to work as a waiter to pay for his tuition. Even so, he ran out of funds after two years and had to quit, becoming editor of a local paper. After a few years and a couple more jobs, Merrill wound up working on Wall Street.

Merrill turned out to have a natural aptitude for the world of finance, and at the age of 29 he set up his own business. Charles E Merrill & Company (he later joined forces with bond salesman Edmund C. Lynch) specialised in investment and merchant banking for the retail industry. Why the retail industry? Because Merrill had foreseen ahead of anyone else that chain stores would be the future of retailing. So he underwrote organisations such as Safeway Stores, McCrory and SS Kresge (which became KMart), and quickly earned himself a fortune. He also predicted the rise of the movie industry, and made himself even richer by financing movie companies.

> ### Charles Merrill ... on priorites
>
> The interests of our customers must come first.

Merrill really made his name, however, after the Crash of 1929, which he was the first major player on Wall Street to predict. He did his best to persuade the President to discourage speculation in the months before the Crash, but Calvin Coolidge wouldn't listen. Eventually Merrill, certain that disaster was approaching, liquidated his company's stock portfolio. His foresight made him famous when the Crash he had predicted finally materialised in October; he had saved his customers an estimated $6 million.

Meanwhile, Merrill had been developing his interests in Safeway, and in 1930 he left the brokerage industry altogether to concentrate on underwriting and banking, and to expand the retail chain, in which he was the major stockholder. His brokerage business was transferred to another company in which he became a silent partner. He concentrated on organising a major and very successful expansion programme for Safeway through mergers, although he appointed a CEO to run the business. By 1953 Safeway was the second largest food chain in the US, and Merrill had also launched *Family Circle* magazine, which was distributed through Safeway, as a money-spinner on the side.

By the end of the 1930s, Merrill had already had two successful careers – one as an investment banker and one as a retail chain owner. And his life was fairly colourful too. Good Time Charlie, as he was known by his friends, had been married and divorced three times, had three children and three homes, and was known for his love of champagne and women. He was an egotistical man, who liked to be the centre of attention, and generally was. His son (Pulitzer Prize-winning poet James Merrill) once wrote of him, 'Whatever he decided to serve, the victim was meant to choke it down and be grateful.'

In 1941 Merrill's partner Lynch died and Merrill returned to brokerage. He merged with several other firms to form the world's largest brokerage house – Merrill, Lynch, Pierce, Fenner and Beane – with 71 partners. He wanted to encourage small investors, with perhaps one or two thousand dollars to play with, to invest in Wall Street. Although other brokers had also felt that Wall Street should be open to a wider market, Merrill was the first successfully to do anything about it.

What he did was to launch a huge campaign to educate and encourage the public to invest their savings effectively. He advertised securities

---

Charles Merrill ... on buying stocks

Investigate, then invest.

---

and printed clearly written, simple guides to investing in the newspapers, taking full-page ads to do it. The response rate to these was about a thousand a day. He held seminars around the country with childcare facilities so both husbands and wives could listen to the presentation. He even gave away stock as a prize in a breakfast cereal competition. In order to build public confidence, he was the first in the industry to publicly disclose an annual performance statement.

At the same time as educating and encouraging the public to invest, Merrill also overhauled the way brokerages worked. He changed the system of paying salesmen from commissions to salaries with profit-sharing, he trained his brokers and directed new customers to the brokers who were most experienced in the investment activities the customer wanted. Other Wall Street brokerages followed suit, but Merrill was in the lead, with a 12 per cent share of all trades on the New York Stock Exchange by 1953.

Merrill suffered a series of heart attacks in 1944 and 1945, after which he went into semi-retirement, but still remained a force in the business. By the time he died in 1956, his company had around 400,000 clients and was the biggest brokerage in the US (and still is). But Merril wasn't satisfied. Although he encouraged thousands of small investors, and many brokerages followed his lead, his success wasn't as overwhelming as he had hoped. The Depression was still too recent a memory for many people and take-up of Merrill's ideas was slow.

Nevertheless, Merrill had brought about a sea change, which simply happened slower than he wished. The likes of Charles Schwab and others were no more than followers of Merrill's ideals when they made private investing the huge industry it is today, and a significant contribution to the national economy. And back in the 1940s, Merrill was giving the same advice that today's brokers do: invest for the long term, understand the companies you buy, and have confidence in stocks in the long term. Gone are the days when the stock market belonged to insiders, and it was Charles Merrill who led the crusade.

JOHN PIERPOINT MORGAN

1837–1913

Organisation: *J P Morgan*

Key idea: *Consolidation*

*'The first thing is character, before money or anything else... a man
I do not trust could not get money from me on all the bonds in Chris-
tendom.'*

A t the start of the 20th century, John Pierpoint Morgan was arguably the most powerful man in the world, and is still considered the most powerful financier ever. His passion for mergers
created America's first billion-dollar corporation in 1901, to
press uproar. The newspapers proclaimed that God created the world,
but it was 'reorganised in 1901 by Morgan'.

Morgan was born in Hartford, Connecticut in 1837. When he was
17, his father Junius Spencer Morgan became a partner of the banking
house George Peabody & Co. in London. When Peabody retired, Morgan Sr took over the firm and renamed it J S Morgan & Co. At 19, John
Pierpoint Morgan joined the business, becoming its US agent. He learnt
a great deal about international finance, and was a successful specula-
tor.

Morgan then set up his own banking firm, which later joined forces
with Drexel to become Drexel, Morgan & Co. He developed an influential position in both domestic and international finance, and began to
back many of the new railroad companies. Morgan was never a crook,
but he learnt many tricks of the trade and knew how to exploit the full
potential of a deal. Morgan was growing extremely wealthy and powerful. He had largely earned his reputation financing the railroad network,
and had won respect for successfully unloading William H. Vanderbilt's
$25 million interest in one of the railroads in a private deal.

The railroad network had expanded fast after the Civil War, but
over-competitive pricing and building strategies had left many of them

---

John Pierpoint Morgan ... on motives

A man generally has two reasons for doing a thing. One that sounds good, and a real one.

---

bankrupt and mergers were frequent – mergers which resulted in over-complicated management structures. Morgan rationalised these companies, by financing and reorganisation. Morgan generated new capital for his clients, taking a healthy investment-banking fee in the process. To look after his investments, Morgan made sure he had a seat on the board of the companies he helped, with the result that he ended up as a director of over 20 railroads.

Morgan's great skills were his brains and his determination. By selling securities, consolidating companies and reorganising the railroads, he built a banking empire second to none. His natural character accounted hugely for his success, too. He had a dominating personality, and one that inspired confidence and trust – an ideal recipe for a banker, especially at the turn of the 20th century. When Morgan's father died in 1890, he took over J S Morgan, merged it with his own company, and renamed it J P Morgan & Company, with branches in Paris and London.

Morgan was famous for lending money only when he trusted the creditor and his business venture. On one occasion the son of one of his old friends asked for a loan for an enterprise Morgan didn't consider reliable enough. Morgan refused him, but said, 'Let me offer you something equally valuable.' He invited the young man to walk by his side across the floor of the New York Stock Exchange. Suddenly his young friend found that even if Morgan wouldn't lend him money, everyone else was falling over themselves to.

Railroads weren't Morgan's only interest, of course. He was a principal investor of the Edison General Electric Company. One of the reasons for his enthusiasm for electricity was that he hoped it would be bad news for Rockefeller and his oil empire – Morgan was no fan of Rockefeller. When the first electric streetlights went on in the financial district of New York, they went on in Morgan's offices too. Morgan's deals gave him effective control of the corporations he financed, making him immensely powerful and influential. (One of the businesses he controlled was the White Star Line, which owned the *Titanic*. Morgan was one of the passengers booked on its fatal voyage who cancelled at the last moment.)

John Pierpoint Morgan ... on compound interest

Compounding is the eighth wonder of the world.

In 1901, Morgan pulled of his greatest coup of all. Like Rockefeller (for all their differences) Morgan believed in consolidating companies. It was a neat way to tidy up an industry, and crush the smaller competitors whose price-cutting tactics Morgan saw as destructive to the industry. He had already consolidated many industries, and now he had decided it was time the steel industry went the same way. So he created US Steel, capitalised at $1.4 billion – the world's first billion-dollar corporation.

Morgan's next tactic was to undermine Carnegie's steel firm so he could buy it up cheaply, but Carnegie held on. Eventually Morgan agreed to pay Carnegie nearly half a billion dollars for his business – a deal he agreed in 15 minutes flat. His bank's fees for underwriting the deal were $11.5 million.

In 1907, the US economy was threatened by a stock market panic, and Wall Street turned to Morgan. He showed no signs of panic whatever, but assembled a team of bankers to raise funding to bail out major banks and corporations. He took on the role of last-resort lender for institutions in trouble, the role that is now taken by the US Federal Reserve. And as the Stock Exchange collapsed, Morgan cobbled together $25 million in the space of a few minutes to keep it afloat.

Morgan was also a notable art collector, doubtless at least as attracted by the investment value of his collection as by its artistic value. He started collecting in the 1890s, round about the time his father died, And by the time of his own death in 1913 he had amassed the largest private collection ever known, including paintings and drawings, sculpture, jewellery and manuscripts. Morgan was a philanthropist and, among other gifts, he donated a large part of his art collection to the Metropolitan Museum of Art in New York.

Morgan's greatest financial legacy, however, was ironically the Federal Reserve System, which was established the year he died, 1913. The 'House of Morgan' had such huge influence over the nation's economy that many people were concerned about his excessive power. True, he had rescued the country from bankruptcy, but that was the cause of discontent rather than gratitude. The financial institutions, the big corporations and the US government were concerned that such power lay in the hands of a private individual rather than the state. They decided that a centralised banking system was needed to make sure no financier ever again had the hold over the economy that Morgan had.

AKIO MORITA

1921–1999

Organisation: *Sony*

Key idea: *Japanese management style*

'We thought if we run our company the Japanese way, we cannot always be successful. So that's why Sony's management concept is a mixture of Japanese and Western concept.'

A kio Morita was one of the key Japanese industrialists who helped to rebuild his country after World War II. He was an entrepreneur – who gave us the portable transistor radio, the home video recorder and the Walkman – and also an inspirational manager. He was one of the leading exponents of the Japanese style of management, and the only one who spent time in America learning a Western approach so he could combine the best of each.

Akio Morita was never meant to be an engineer. As far as his father was concerned, he was supposed to take over the family's 400-year-old sake brewing business. But Morita's mother was a fan of Western classical music and had a phonograph machine, and Morita developed an interest in electronics and sound reproduction. In fact, he spent most of his spare time tinkering with various appliances, and taking them apart.

Morita ended up studying physics at Osaka Imperial University, just as the world was going to war. When he graduated he became a Navy lieutenant. After the war he was on the verge of joining the Tokyo Institute of Technology when he read an article about his old Navy colleague, Masara Ibuka. The article said that Ibuka had founded the Tokyo Telecommunications Research Institute in order to generate a new beginning for the country. Morita decided to visit Ibuka, and the two of them decided to start a company together.

Morita, now aged 25, and Ibuka launched their business in 1946 in the ruins of an old department store. They had 20 employees making various products including parts for radios. Technological research and development was Ibuka's speciality, while Morita took charge of marketing and management. Morita was aware that the words 'made in Japan' were synonymous in the West with cheap, tacky goods, and he was determined to change this image. He wanted his brand to be, as Morita put it, the Cadillac of electronics. He also wanted to market goods under his own brand name, unlike the other Japanese manufacturers of the time; Sanyo, for example, was making products for Sears, and Pentax for Honeywell. From the start, Morita was planning a global business.

In 1949, the company developed magnetic recording tape – not an easy task. Morita and Ibuka had to scour Tokyo's black market for oxalic ferrite, which they cooked in a pan to produce ferric oxide. This then had to be brushed by hand onto 30 yards of quarter-inch wide paper. But the end result was the first tape recorder, which went on sale in 1950.

In 1957 Morita came up with another innovation: the pocket transistor radio. In fact, it was a little too large to fit in the average pocket, but that didn't ruffle a creative salesman like Morita. He simply ordered custom made shirts with large pockets for his entire domestic and US sales force. The company sold a million and a half of the radios, many of them in America.

It was the real start of Morita's career as a global brand builder. Morita had the vision to realise that the world was shrinking, and it was only a matter of time before markets became truly international. And he knew he wanted his brand name to be recognisable around the world. At the time, the company was called Tokyo Tsushin Kogyo KK, and you didn't have to possess Morita's instinct for marketing to see that this was hardly a name to conjure with. So he and Ibuka decided to come up with a new brand name.

Morita already had some ideas about the new name. It would have to be recognisable, short, catchy and in Roman letters. After looking through dictionaries, he and Ibuka found the Latin word for sound, *sonus*, and fancied incorporating it into their new name. Not dissimilar was the word sonny, which was popular with young Americans at the time, and which they thought suggested a young, vibrant company. So they combined the two words to create their new name, Sony.

The proposed name change actually met a lot of opposition inside and outside the company, since the existing name had built a wide recognition. But Morita was confident, and the name was changed despite the resistance.

Soon Sony had made the first transistor TV, along with numerous other innovative products. Like his US contemporary Edwin Land, Morita didn't want to enter markets that were already crowded. He

Akio Morita ... on people

You can be totally rational with a machine. But if you work with people, sometimes logic has to take a back seat to understanding.

wanted to create new markets, and his talent for seeing market needs that even the customers themselves weren't aware of is legendary. Morita believed in leading consumer tastes rather than responding to them. The classic example of this is the Walkman.

Morita always maintained that the idea of the Sony Walkman would have been rejected from the start if people had been asked in advance whether they wanted it. But Morita had watched his children playing music all day, and seen people listening in their cars and on the streets – carrying their ghetto blasters with them. Sony's engineers were reluctant to produce a tape player with no recording function, but Morita was adamant. He insisted on a player small enough to be fully portable.

Morita wanted to give his new product the same name around the world – it was central to his global concept of marketing. But the Americans thought Walkman was grammatically poor English so they changed the name to Soundabout. It was changed to Freestyle in Sweden and Stowaway in Britain. Sales were not as good as Sony had hoped, so Morita trusted his instincts and changed the name back to Walkman worldwide. The product was a legendary success, and the word Walkman can even be found in some dictionaries.

In 1960, Sony established Sony Corporation of America, and Morita decided to move his family to the US, a step which had never occurred to other Japanese business leaders. On his return, he applied many American business principles to running Sony. However, he felt US businesses took far too short-term a view, something Morita could never be accused of, having planned in 1946 to expand his new start-up around the world.

Morita advocated many Japanese business practices, especially the traditional care for employees, and he felt that the West was too concerned with financial games and paper assets, while the Japanese set more store – rightly in his view – on developing real products with lasting value. But he took on board more Western attitudes too, such as the culture of reward-sharing, where employees earn better salaries and benefits, and shareholders receive bigger dividends. Not only should companies look after their employees in the traditional Japanese style,

---

Akio Morita ... on where the buck stops

If we face a recession, we should not lay off employees; the company should sacrifice a profit. It's management's risk and management's responsibility. Employees are not guilty; why should they suffer?

---

but they should also aim to improve their quality of life in the Western tradition too.

Morita was a popular leader among his staff, and inspired great loyalty. He had a gentle charisma and a cheerful disposition, and a zest for new experiences: he was well over 50 when he learnt to ski and to scuba dive, and he was still playing tennis regularly into his 70s.

In 1989 Sony bought Columbia Pictures, with the result that the company had more foreigners than Japanese on its payroll; Morita had taken his organisation way beyond Japan's borders, as he had always intended to. Morita suffered a stroke in 1993 and resigned as chairman of Sony, leaving a company with annual sales of well over $30 billion. Morita died in 1999, aged 78; the obituaries hailed him as one of the most influential industrialists of the century.

DAVID OGILVY
1911–1999

Organisation: *Ogilvy & Mather*

Key idea: *Brand building*

'Only first class businesses, and that in a first-class way.'

O ne of the most famous names in advertising, David Ogilvy was 37 before he launched his business, with little experience of the advertising industry. In fact, he gave up being an Amish farmer to start an advertising agency. It didn't take him long, however, to become extremely well known for his memorable and effective ad campaigns. But as well as possessing rare creative talent, Ogilvy also knew how to build a business. So he should; his campaigns helped increase sales for countless clients. Applying to his own company the same brand-building skills he sold to his clients, he turned Ogilvy & Mather into the fourth-largest advertising agency in the world.

Ogilvy was born and grew up in England and Scotland. His father was somewhat eccentric, but determined to breed guts and intelligence into the boy. To this end, he gave his son a glass of raw blood to drink each day from the age of six, and required him to eat calves' brains three times a week, washed down with beer. Ogilvy certainly ended up with both guts and brains, though whether he actually achieved them through the diet his father laid down for him might be questionable.

Ogilvy was a successful student until he arrived at Oxford, where he was eventually thrown out (as he put it); he considered it the one real failure of his life. Ogilvy then launched in to a string of highly varied jobs, many of which honed his fast-developing skills as a salesman. He worked as a chef in Paris, then returned to England and sold Aga ovens door-to-door.

In 1936, aged 25, Ogilvy had his first brush with the world of advertising when his brother got him a job at the London agency Mather & Crowley. This meant going to the US for a year to study American advertising methods. Shortly after returning to England, Ogilvy decided to emigrate to the US, so in 1938 he found himself back in America as associate director of George Gallup's Audience Research Institute. After three years learning about research, Ogilvy put his skills to use intelligence gathering for the British government during the war. At the end of World War II, Ogilvy opted for yet another career change and tried his hand (unsuccessfully) as a tobacco farmer in the Amish community in Pennsylvania.

Ogilvy now moved to New York and decided to launch his own advertising agency. He had only $6000, however, which was hardly enough. So he drummed up backing from Mather & Crowley, and another London agency named SH Benson who insisted he hire someone who knew how to run an advertising agency. Ogilvy found an accountant named Anderson Hewitt, and he was ready to launch his agency: Hewitt, Ogilvy, Benson & Mather.

Over 30 years later, Ogilvy sent one of his partners a memo which read:

> *'Will Any Agency Hire This Man?*
>
> *'He is 38, and unemployed. He dropped out of college. He has been a cook, a salesman, a diplomatist and a farmer. He knows nothing about marketing and has never written any copy. He professes to be interested in advertising as a career (at the age of 38!) and is ready to go to work for $5000 a year. I doubt if any American agency will hire him.*
>
> *'However, a London agency did hire him. Three years later he became the most famous copywriter in the world, and in due course built the tenth biggest agency in the world.*
>
> *'The moral: it sometimes pays an agency to be imaginative and unorthodox in hiring. D.O.'*

Ogilvy knew that to succeed, his agency needed a strong brand image. As an ex-patriate Englishman heading up a small offshoot of a British firm, he reckoned his agency should be seen as respectable, high quality, intelligent and highly creative. As chief salesman he had no trouble projecting this image: he himself was an intelligent, flamboyant but gentlemanly character, full of charisma and with a disarming combination of creativity and plain common sense.

Ogilvy was going to specialise in brand advertising for businesses with a high-quality image. His job was to provide advertising that would generate sales, and he was certain that brand advertising was the best way to build those sales. Never short on confidence, he was convinced

David Ogilvy ... on leadership

There appears to be no correlation between leadership and academic achievement. I was relieved to learn this, because I have no college degree. The motivation which makes a man a good student is not the kind of motivation which makes him a good leader.

that down-to-earth, plain-spoken advertising was the type that worked. He had no time for clever or gimmicky campaigns. Advertising was a medium for information, not an art form.

With his clear vision of his own brand and his own style, Ogilvy began to tout for business. As a natural salesman, it didn't take him long to find it. After three years, the agency had achieved sales of around $9 million, and Ogilvy devised a couple of hugely successful campaigns, for Hathaway shirts and Schweppes soft drinks, which won him and his agency a name for themselves. Ogilvy was beginning to become famous in his field. His partner, Hewitt, was left out of the limelight altogether, and soon opted out of the company, which now became Ogilvy, Benson & Mather. But it was Ogilvy's next big campaign that was the clincher as far as his reputation was concerned.

Rolls Royce approached him with a mere $50,000 advertising budget, wanting Ogilvy to come up with an ad for their new model. This was exactly the kind of high-quality client that Ogilvy wanted, and he was delighted. He wrote them an ad which was so effective it became arguably the most famous car ad headline ever: 'At 60 miles an hour, the loudest noise in the new Rolls Royce comes from the electric clock.'

Ogilvy, Benson & Mather was now rated as one of the most creative agencies, and had a fast-growing reputation. Over the next 15 years or so Ogilvy pulled in contracts from American Express, Lever Brothers, Shell and General Foods among many others, gradually building the business until it had offices in 17 countries by 1970.

Of course, one man can't write all that copy and run all those campaigns. But Ogilvy didn't have to. He managed to do something even better. He developed and nurtured creative talent wherever he could find it, so that he could fill his offices with ad executives all with the same clear focus as he had. He made sure their focus was the same as his by endlessly reiterating his guidelines on what advertising was all about, and insisting that knowledge – of the product and of the market – was the key to good advertising. Ogilvy circulated memos and gave speeches

---

David Ogilvy ... on success

If you want to follow my example, here is the recipe: First, make a reputation for being a creative genius. Second, surround yourself with partners who are better than you are. Third, leave them to get on with it.

---

reinforcing his guidelines for good, clear, effective advertising. Classic Ogilvy bite-sized advice included:

- Big ideas are usually simple ideas.
- The consumer's not a moron, she's your wife. Don't insult her intelligence.
- Never run an ad you wouldn't want your family to see.

Ogilvy also had a talent for spotting people with potential, and hiring them. Not only did he hire the best himself, he taught his management staff to do the same. He reminded them, 'Ogilvy & Mather does two things: we look after clients and we teach young advertising people.' Whenever he appointed an office head, he sent them a set of Russian dolls. Inside the smallest one he put a note which read, 'If each of us hires people who are smaller than we are, we shall become a company of *dwarfs*, but if each of us hires people who are bigger than we are, Ogilvy & Mather will become a company of *giants*.'

In 1965, Ogilvy merged his agency with Mather & Crowther, and the following year became one of the first ad agencies to go public. In 1973 he retired as chairman, although he stayed in regular touch with the agency. In 1989 The Ogilvy Group was sold to WPP, making WPP it the largest marketing communications firm in the world – Ogilvy spent the next three years as the organisation's non-executive chairman before finally retiring to France.

TONY O'REILLY

1936–

Organisation: *Heinz*

Key idea: *Promotion*

'The whole world is your competition now.'

Tony O'Reilly was appointed MD of H J Heinz, England at the age of 33, an ex-international rugby player and an Irishman. Ten years later he was CEO of H J Heinz's international operations. He went on to become the first non-family member to serve as chairman of the company .So what qualified him to run an organisation like Heinz?

O'Reilly was born and educated in Dublin, graduating in law from University College, Dublin. Among other educational achievements, he also earned a PhD in agricultural marketing from Bradford University. Meantime, he played rugby, earning 29 caps for his country. He was part of the winning teams that toured South Africa in 1955, and New Zealand and Australia in 1959, and was a driving force behind the success of both.

After completing his education, O'Reilly worked as an industrial consultant, and then became chairman of the Irish Dairy Board at the age of 26, where he brought the country's dairy products to a wider market, and developed the brand 'Kerrygold'. He then spent three years with the Irish Sugar Company before he was drafted in to run Heinz's UK operation, its largest subsidiary outside the US. He worked his way up the organisation to become President and Chief Operating Officer of Heinz worldwide in 1973, at the age of 37.

When O'Reilly took over as CEO in 1979, H J Heinz's market capitalisation was $908 million. By the time he stepped down as Chairman in 1998, it was $19 billion. O'Reilly adopted the tactics of a rugby player to take Heinz to the level of a truly international player. Although the organisation was already operating worldwide, he vastly increased the brand's recognition around the globe, especially in expanding into

Tony O'Reilly ... on brand loyalty

The acid test of brand loyalty is whether a housewife intending to buy Heinz Tomato Ketchup in a store, finding it to be out of stock, will walk out of the store to buy it elsewhere or switch to an alternative product.

Africa, Eastern Europe, China and the Pacific Rim. O'Reilly hit the ground running, and brought vast energy to the job. He was a clever tactician, and he wasn't afraid to beat off the competition fiercely.

O'Reilly is a man of massive charisma and enthusiasm; one of those who sleeps only half as long at night as the rest of us. Henry Kissinger once said of him, 'If we could imagine in business the same talent as the Renaissance's tradesmen, this would describe Tony O'Reilly.' His key strategies were to acquire overseas companies to build up the organisation's global influence, and to hire in the best people no matter what the cost. He put vast resources into advertising and promoting the Heinz brand, along with its other products – only 30 per cent of Heinz products carry the Heinz name. It was O'Reilly's mission to spread the gospel of Heinz and its products to the world.

One of O'Reilly's smartest acquisitions was Weight Watchers International, which he then built up into the largest weight loss programme in the US. Heinz's other brand names include StarKist, Farley's and many more, spanning over 4000 products (so much for the famous 57 varieties). O'Reilly responded to the new environmentally aware shopper ahead of most corporations, and StarKist introduced the world's first dolphin-friendly tuna. O'Reilly also spearheaded the idea of the 'ecological oasis' for the farm-to-factory production of Heinz baby foods. During his boom time at Heinz, O'Reilly gave shareholders a 22 per cent annual return.

O'Reilly took over a company that had had an amazing run of superb leaders, from Henry J. Heinz himself onwards. But he still managed to expand the business out of all proportion to expectations. This is why his board continued to support him even when he began to be held up as an example, in the nineties, of a grossly overpaid CEO. When restructuring meant laying off workers, O'Reilly was still taking home a vast salary.

O'Reilly's shares in Heinz made him a billionaire, and he is famous for the parties he throws at his castle in Ireland, and for mixing with politicians and Hollywood stars. Far from retiring when he left Heinz

> ## Tony O'Reilly ... on the Internet
>
> The verb to browse is completely misapplied to the Internet.

(at the age of 62), he continued to pursue his other business interests. His Irish companies – which include Independent Newspapers plc – are worth $20 billion. Among the key people in these organisations are several of his children; perhaps like Henry J. Heinz before him he is starting a business dynasty.

Like so many inspirational leaders, O'Reilly is very active in charitable organisations, and chairs the Ireland Funds of many countries, including the US, Great Britain and Australia. These funds have raised millions towards programmes that encourage peace and reconciliation throughout Ireland.

DAVID PACKARD

1912–1996

Organisation: *Hewlett-Packard*

Key idea: *Managing By Walking About (MBWA)*

'Our company philosophy [is] to grow as fast as we can with our own earnings and make every job we create a permanent one.'

D avid Packard, together with Bill Hewlett, built up a company from just about nothing to a massive organisation with revenues of over $30 billion. Not only that, but their company became one of the most liked and admired in America, held up as an example of innovation, good employee relations and excellent leadership. The key to Hewlett-Packard's success was the simplicity of its approach. The way they did things became known as the HP Way – also the title of Packard's 1995 book.

David Packard came from a comfortable home in Colorado. At ten years of age he decided he wanted to be an engineer, and he never faltered in his resolve. He studied engineering at Stanford University in Palo Alto, where he met Bill Hewlett, who became a great friend and who shared Packard's interest in electrical engineering. By the time they graduated, the Depression had sobered them along with everyone else, and they wanted to find steady work. So they started their own company. According to Packard, 'We thought we would have a job for ourselves. That's all we thought about in the beginning. We hadn't the slightest idea of building a big company.'

In 1937, Packard and Hewlett set themselves up with $538 and a rented garage in Palo Alto – the place where the phenomenon that is Silicon Valley would eventually grow up around them. They began by hiring themselves out as inventors, but soon began developing their own products. Their first profitable invention was a sound machine to help engineers make clear recordings. More followed, and by the end of their first year the pair had earned themselves a profit of $1300.

Business grew fast, and in 1940 Hewlett-Packard left the garage behind. Things went well during the war, and the firm employed almost 150 people at its height. But after the war, sales dropped by half. Hewlett and Packard responded by hiring in technical talent. The strategy worked, and within two years the business was turning over more than $2 million. It never looked back, thanks to the innovative and entrepreneurial culture that Packard and Hewlett maintained.

During the war, Hewlett had served with the Signal Corps, leaving Packard to oversee the running of the business. On Hewlett's return, he opted to exercise his engineering skills by taking charge of product planning, leaving Packard to become a professional manager. He turned out to have a unique and effective approach.

Packard wasn't interested in the trappings of power, and had an open-door policy throughout the company. Employees were welcome to talk to him about problems or bring him questions. He believed managers – himself included – should be visible and available, a system of management he called Managing By Walking About (a term coined by one of his managers).

Employees were given as much responsibility as possible, and treated with trust and respect. He said, 'The most important element in our personnel policy is the degree to which we are able to get over to our people that we have faith in them … We figured that people would accomplish more if they were given an opportunity to use their talents and abilities in the way they work best. How do you do this? You establish some objectives for them, provide some incentive, and try not to direct the detailed way in which they do their work.'

Employee loyalty at Hewlett-Packard has always been tremendously high, as a result of Packard's culture of trust and respect for them. When the US economy slumped in 1970, orders were below production capacity. The standard response to this was to lay off staff. But Packard was never very interested in the standard industry response to things. So he did it differently. With the co-operation of the staff (many of whom owned company stock and were therefore motivated to keep the business profitable) they worked only nine days instead of ten in every two weeks, and everyone took a 10 per cent pay cut. That went for everyone, from top executives down.

After six months, order levels returned to normal and everyone was back at work full time. Some people even said they had enjoyed the longer weekends, despite the reduction in pay. Packard explained, 'The net result … was that effectively all shared the burden of the recession,

David Packard ... on organisation

You've got to avoid having too rigid an organisation. When you get up to a certain size you need to have some sort of structure. So you work out an organisation chart that gives people areas of responsibility. You make sure that all the areas are covered and relate properly to each other.

Actually, if an organisation is going to work effectively the communications should be through the most effective channel regardless of the organisation chart. I've often thought that after you get organised you ought to throw the chart away.

good people were not released into a very tough job market, and we had our highly qualified workforce in place when business improved.'

Not only was Packard's attitude to employees effective and highly motivating, his business strategy was also refreshing. He had no time for conventional business practices right from the start. When discussing the early years of Hewlett-Packard he commented, 'Professors of management are devastated when I say we were successful because we had no plans. We just took on odd jobs.' In the 1970s, he railed against the accepted theory that businesses should strive for greater market share: 'Somewhere we got into the idea that market share was an objective. I hope that's straightened out. Anyone can build market share, and if you set your prices low enough, you can get the whole damn market. But I'll tell you it won't get you anywhere around here ...'

Packard didn't like taking big financial risks, and he disapproved of long-term borrowing: 'My philosophy goes back to the Depression. I don't want to be in debt if a downturn comes.' This steady, solid financial approach made Hewlett-Packard a rarity in the volatile world of Silicon Valley.

Hewlett-Packard's management structure and systems were always very simple. When a division got too big – around 1500 people – they would split it up so it didn't become too unwieldy. The company spent very little time navel-gazing or congratulating itself on its success; they all just rolled up their sleeves and got on with the job.

By the 1980s, Hewlett-Packard's constant innovation had made it America's fourth largest computer manufacturer. But by 1990 its profits started to drop, and it was falling behind the competition – it was no longer innovating faster than the rest of them as it had done before.

David Packard ... on trust

[Hewlett-Packard had a policy of keeping storerooms unlocked and parts bins open. One reason was that the easy access helped designers and others who wanted to work on ideas at home or at weekends.]

A second reason, less tangible but important, is that the open bins and storerooms were a symbol of trust, a trust that is central to the way HP does business.

Packard and Hewlett were by now in their late 70s, but they nevertheless had to fight the young entrepreneurs of Silicon Valley to regain their position. They started by doing what they did best: Managing By Walking About. They talked to as many employees as they could, at all levels. And they discovered that they had too many layers and committees. The problem had been building slowly and insidiously, and the corporate structure had become too cumbersome to move fast.

Packard and Hewlett's response was to cut down management to only four layers between Packard and just about any of his employees, and to make work teams smaller and more autonomous, to give the business back its entrepreneurial edge. Development time for new products was halved, and by 1992 Hewlett-Packard was moving faster again than the rest of the industry.

Packard retired in 1993, leaving a business that is remarkable for its combination of the traditional and the forward thinking. Packard combined an almost old-fashioned attitude to finance and risk, and a paternal attitude to employees, with an innovative entrepreneurship which pervades the entire company, and which means it is still one of the leading forces in Silicon Valley.

JOHN REITH (LORD REITH)

1889–1971

Organisation: *BBC*

Key idea: *Public service broadcasting*

*'The purpose of broadcasting in the public interest is to inform, edu-
cate and entertain.'*

C uriously enough John Reith, the founder of British broadcasting, had little time for television, which he considered deeply
inferior to radio. He saw its application as limited by comparison and yet – despite being proved wrong in his assessment –
his influence on television was so great that it persists to this day. Reith
was an engineer by profession, not a broadcaster (there had never been
such a thing as a broadcaster when he started at the BBC), yet he quickly
saw that the new medium of radio was not about engineering but about
communicating.

Reith was the fifth son of a Scottish Calvinist minister, who instilled
in him a strong sense of public duty. Reith grew up with firm Christian
beliefs which stayed with him, and which he incorporated into the ethos
of the BBC (the chief engineer in 1929 had to resign because he was
named in a divorce case). He trained in engineering at the Glasgow
Academy, and then joined the army in 1911. He was badly wounded during World War I and his face was scarred for life.

After the war, Reith worked for a while in America, where he picked
up an American outlook in terms of pragmatism and positive thinking.
He returned to England and was starting to get bored with a career in
engineering when, in 1922, he saw two job advertisements that caught
his eye. One was looking for people to build a railway system in the Amazon, and the other was an advertisement for a post at the newly started
BBC. He applied for both jobs, and was offered both. He knew nothing
about radio – he didn't even own a wireless – but he can't have known
that much about living in the Amazon either. In any case, he opted for

the BBC job. A year later he was managing director, with a team of four staff under him.

The BBC was a commercial operation at the time, but Reith was committed to public service broadcasting – a subject on which he quickly formed extremely firm views. He insisted that the corporation must be motivated by public service and not commercial considerations, that it should give national coverage from a central operation, not from local stations, and that the standards of programming must be as high as possible. Although his background was in engineering, he was fast becoming an expert in communication. His approach to broadcasting stayed with the BBC for decades after Reith left, and in many ways it still influences the BBC today.

Reith was keen to identify the BBC with the political establishment, although he was determined that it shouldn't give up its independence. Despite government pressure, Reith refused to take sides against the strikers during the 1926 General Strike. In 1927, the BBC became a public corporation, and its charter stipulated that the BBC must not broadcast any material that the government deemed controversial. Reith was insistent that impartiality was more important, and fought to have this restriction lifted – his campaign succeeded a year later. The independence of the BBC, championed by Reith, is still one of its greatest strengths.

Reith's insistence on the highest possible standards meant working with the best writers, performers and directors, promoting British culture, and pioneering new and important artistic work. Reith was a great visionary, and knew exactly what he wanted the BBC to be. He effectively invented public service broadcasting, designing a model that has been copied around the world.

Reith was also extremely skilled at buttering up the establishment. Not long after he became Director General of the BBC, he realised that he needed key establishment figures on his side to promote the new wireless technology. So he invited the Archbishop of Canterbury and his wife for dinner at his own house. The guests were astounded to hear the radio playing in the dining room (the Archbishop's wife was amazed the radio waves could get in through the closed windows), but the Archbishop felt the loud symphony that was playing didn't sit well with dinner. So Reith, making his excuses to leave the room, telephoned Broadcasting House and arranged for the symphony to be followed by a Schubert piano sonata.

It was also Reith who spent three patient years persuading King George V to use the new radio technology to broadcast directly to his

> ## Lord Reith ... on keeping the public interested
>
> Radio provides the quickest possible exit for the largest number of people in the shortest possible time.

people. After much resistance, the King was finally persuaded and instituted the tradition of the Christmas broadcast.

Reith was an inspired leader with a clear vision, but he was not an easy man. For a start, he was almost always certain he was right. At an early age he wrote in his diary, 'I was not meant to be a mediocrity', and in a later diary (he was a copious diarist) he wrote 'What a curse it is to have outstanding comprehensive ability and intelligence, combined with the drive to use them to maximum purpose'. Reith was an irascible, autocratic character, known by his subordinates as 'Mussolini'. Although he gave the BBC as an organisation great energy and direction, staff morale was often low under his control.

Reith was also a reactionary in many ways, and imposed his increasingly outmoded morals on BBC output. He tried to ban the Charleston from the BBC, and he banned one violinist from playing on the radio because she was a divorcee. And he had little time for television, not seeing its potential, and was far from co-operative with the likes of John Logie Baird. However, he eventually oversaw the launch of the world's first public scheduled television broadcasts in 1936.

By the late 1930s Reith was getting bored at the BBC. He had created the organisation from virtually nothing, given it vision and direction, and now felt there was nothing left to do with it but tinker. The boredom was mutual, as many staff and others involved with the organisation were getting fed up with his self-righteous moral inflexibility. In 1938, Reith was ousted from the BBC by its board of governors, supported by the government. He was extremely bitter about it, despite the fact that he was probably ready to go in any case.

Reith never again achieved the great success he had at the BBC. He moved to Imperial Airways, which he ran for a couple of years, and followed this with a series of jobs in business and politics, having been created a baron in 1940. He held several minor cabinet posts during World War II and afterwards.

Despite his great vision of the future of public service broadcasting, Reith was unable to move with the times. Inflexibly opposed to commercialism in broadcasting, Reith fought the introduction of commercial television. Speaking against it in the Lords in 1952, he argued,

Lord Reith ... on moral responsibility

Broadcasting must be conducted as a public service with definite standards ... the preservation of a high moral tone is of paramount importance.

'Somebody introduced dog-racing into England... And somebody introduced smallpox, bubonic plague and the Black Death. Somebody is minded now to introduce sponsored broadcasting into this country.'

ALF ROBENS
1910–1999

Organisation: *National Coal Board*

Key idea: *Great Britain Ltd*

'We should never be allowed to forget that it is the customer who, in the end, determines how many people are employed and what sort of wages companies can afford.'

Alf Robens was very nearly leader of the Labour Party, which would most likely have led to his becoming Prime Minister. But somehow fate saw to it that he missed out on his first choice of job. Instead, he had a chance to put many of his principles into practice as chairman of the National Coal Board, which he transformed during the 1960s. He believed that even a nationalised industry could only succeed if it was run like a commercial business, and he proved he was right.

Robens grew up in Manchester where he went to school until he was 15. He left to work in a shop selling umbrellas, and then moved into marketing at the Co-op. By the age of 25 he was working full time for the shop workers' union. Ten years later he stood for parliament as a member of the Labour Party, and was part of their landslide victory of 1945. He represented a Northumberland constituency in a traditional mining area.

Robens was highly respected by his party, and quickly moved up the ladder to become a junior minister at the Ministry of Fuel and Power, and then Minister of Labour. But in 1951, the Labour Party was ousted and Robens found himself in opposition. He was tipped as a future leader of the party but he wasn't happy away from the centre of power, and he disliked the infighting in his party under Gaitskell. So he accepted the invitation Macmillan gave him in 1961 to become chairman of the National Coal Board. No doubt he was encouraged by the offer of a life peerage that went with it, and he promised Gaitskell he

> ## Alf Robens ... on safety at work
>
> Safety belongs to all workplaces, not just a production site.

would return to a future Labour government as a minister. Only two years later Gaitskell died; it's very possible that had Robens stayed in parliament he might have become party leader.

As it was, he found himself with a coal board to run: an inefficient dinosaur of a coal board. It was heavily bureaucratic and employed too many management staff and too many miners below ground – 600,000 employees in all. It was being threatened by cheap oil and, before long, North Sea gas and nuclear power would put even greater pressure on it. Robens' mission was to make it more profitable.

The general feeling in nationalised industries at the time was that the government owed jobs to the workers. Robens, however, despite being a Labour politician, was on the centre right of his party and held more pragmatic views. He believed that what the country needed was to stop following outdated political patterns and to behave more like a business corporation – Great Britain Ltd as he termed it.

Robens might have lost his chance to run the country, but he still had the Coal Board to practise his policies on. And they were very much in tune with the times – people liked his approach and wanted to see it work. Robens believed that the Coal Board's problems could be solved by applying management techniques, so that's what he did. He adopted a three-pronged attack to drag the organisation into modernity: he battled the competition from oil and other sources of power with a massive sales campaign, he streamlined management and administration, and he mechanised as much of the operation as possible.

Robens knew that this would entail considerable job losses – eventually more than half the workforce would have to go. So he needed to keep the workers on his side. He began by acquiring (despite much criticism) an aeroplane so that he could visit the coalmines and other sites frequently. The workers may have thought his mode of transport unnecessarily flash and expensive, but they appreciated the fact that he turned up at the mines.

One of the issues of conflict at the time was the practice of paying miners piecework instead of daily wages. Robens earned the appreciation of the miners by changing the system over to day wages. He also made sure that those who were necessarily made redundant at least received generous redundancy payments. Although the most militant

---

Alf Robens ... on Great Britain Ltd

... with a damned good chairman and managing director, and a damned good board.

---

union members were in frequent conflict with Robens, the majority of miners respected him and recognised that he had no option but to lay off workers. It was only towards the very end of his tenure that he met with any significant industrial action.

Robens spent ten years at the National Coal Board, during which time productivity rose by over 50 per cent, and the number of pits dropped by more than half to only 300. He was also one of the most powerful political figures of the time, whose advice was widely sought and taken. In the mid-1960s, Robens was surprised to find that the newly elected Labour government was less sympathetic to his views than the outgoing Tories had been. Nevertheless, his enormous achievement turning a nationalised industry into a commercial venture had earned him huge political clout.

Robens was not a modest man, and in a way it was his undoing. Despite an excellent achievement at the Coal Board his name is largely associated by many people with his behaviour after the Aberfan disaster. In 1966, a huge mountain of slurry cascaded down from a Coal Board tip and buried the village school at Aberfan. 116 children and 28 adults died; the village lost an entire generation of its children. Robens was told immediately about the disaster but decided to keep his existing appointment that day – being installed as Chancellor of Surrey University – rather than go to Wales to visit the scene of the tragedy. In the resulting backlash against him Robens tendered his resignation, but it was refused.

When the Conservatives came to power in 1970, they invited Robens to stay on at the Coal Board. However, he could see that since they wanted to wind down the nationalised industries, he was hardly going to find opportunities for expanding it as he wanted to. So he declined the offer. Instead, he left to take on a series of successful chairmanships and directorships, including becoming chairman of the Engineering Industries Council. He wrote a report on health and safety at work in 1972, known as the Robens Report, which influenced employment law not only in the UK but also in Australia, Sweden, Canada and parts of the US as well.

Robens died in 1999, having claimed that he never regretted taking the job at the National Coal Board. But despite his success there, he must have wondered what might have happened if he had become leader of the Labour Party. As he himself had said, 'I yearned to be Prime Minister.'

JOHN D. ROCKEFELLER

1839–1937

Organisation: *Standard Oil*

Key idea: *The giant corporation*

'The man who starts out simply with the idea of getting rich won't succeed; you must have a larger ambition.'

John D. Rockefeller is probably most famous for being the world's first billionaire; for a long time he was the world's only billionaire. His first job earned him just $10 a week. At the height of his fortune he was worth $9 billion. By the time he died, however, he had given away so much that he was worth a mere $26 million. What's more, by that time he had been retired for 40 years.

Rockefeller was not a charismatic personality, nor a classic salesman, but he had a combination of talents that enabled him to build up an organisation so huge that eventually the Ohio courts insisted it be broken up. He created a whole new approach to industry which, although it runs counter to modern principles of free trade, nevertheless laid the foundations for modern big business corporations.

John D. Rockefeller's father sold patent medicines and spent a lot of time travelling. His mother ran the home, and was deeply religious and disciplined. She taught her children to work hard, save money and give to charity – something her son would later do on an unprecedented scale. All these principles, in fact, played an important role in Rockefeller's career.

By the time he was 12, the young Rockefeller had saved over $50 from doing odd jobs locally. His mother persuaded him to lend the entire sum to a neighbouring farmer at seven per cent interest, repayable in one year. When his money returned to him Rockefeller got his first taste of growing his own business.

He left school at 16, and visited every business in Cleveland, Ohio – where the family lived – to find work. Eventually he was employed as a clerk with a commission merchant and produce shipper called Hewitt & Tuttle. He turned out to be a thorough, diligent and honest worker, and began to move up the company. He learnt to be polite and pleasant but persistent in collecting overdue accounts. Throughout his life he was known for his pleasant manner – he never swore or raised his voice – and he always said he first learnt to be patient with people during his time at Hewitt & Tuttle. He claimed patience and courage were the secrets of his success: 'You can abuse me, you can strike me, so long as you let me have my own way.'

In 1859, still aged only 19, Rockerfeller went into partnership with a neighbour named Maurice Clark. They set up as produce wholesalers, to immediate success. This success was largely due to Rockefeller's business acumen. He was extremely diligent and paid great attention to detail, and would weigh the arguments carefully before going into any deal. However, unexpectedly for such a careful person, once he had decided to do a deal he would see it through at all costs with iron determination. In fact, the risks he was prepared to take once his mind was set could be quite nerve-wracking for his associates.

But it was dawning on Rockefeller that the wholesale business in Ohio was never going to grow that big. The railroads were coming, and they would undermine Cleveland's transportation advantage as a lake port. The goods he dealt in would be moved around by train in future. He needed to find another product, one for which Cleveland's position halfway between the Atlantic coast and Chicago would be an advantage.

Rockefeller was looking for a new industry to move into and in 1863, he struck oil. Literally. Small oil refineries had been springing up for a few years, all of them slightly shabby, disorderly businesses. Rockefeller saw an opportunity for someone who could apply thorough, methodical business methods to the industry. The first oilfields were in Pennsylvania, and Rockefeller also realised that Cleveland was superbly located for positioning an oil refinery, with its railroad routes straight into New York.

Rockefeller and Clark, along with three other partners, set up Andrews, Clark & Co and went into the oil refining business. By 1865 the partners were falling out over the management of their business so they decided to sell the refinery to whichever of them made the highest bid. Rockefeller bought it for $72,500.

The oil industry expanded, and Rockefeller's company expanded along with it. Unlike the other shoddy refineries of the time, his were well built and he invested heavily in them. With his attention to detail and his hatred of waste, he aimed for optimum efficiency. So he hired his

John D. Rockefeller ... on focus

We devoted ourselves exclusively to the oil business and its products. The company never went into outside ventures, but kept to the enormous task of perfecting its own organisation.

own plumber, and set up his own cooperage to make the barrels for his oil. He even bought timber plantations to make the barrels, and dried the timber out on site so it was lighter – and therefore cheaper – to transport than if he dried it out when it reached the cooperage. His thoroughness in saving every penny was legendary. He once spoke to a man soldering the tops on to metal barrels and asked him how many drops of solder he used per barrel. 'Forty,' replied the man. Rockefeller replied, 'Have you tried thirty-eight?'

Rockefeller was a strange contradiction. On the one hand this thorough, careful man wanted to save the cost of a drop of solder on each barrel. And yet, when it came to building his business, he was the most daring borrower, always looking for loans to finance his latest expansion plans. He had many business partners, most of whom dropped out of the business sooner or later because they couldn't face the financial risks Rockefeller seemed happy to take daily.

In 1869, Rockefeller decided to incorporate the company in order to reduce his dependence on loans. By now he had bought up many smaller refineries and his was the largest oil refining company in the world. He formed the Standard Oil Company, and continued to buy up as many other refineries as he could. And he continued to streamline his operations, as Standard Oil set up its own cooperages and warehouses, bought in its own hoop iron, manufactured its own sulphuric acid (to use in the refining process) and reduced its costs wherever possible. Economy of scale soon meant that no new players in the industry could hope to compete.

In 1882, all of Standard Oil's interests were merged into the Standard Oil Trust. Rockefeller believed that free competition didn't work when there were numerous large, medium and small firms, since the small firms drove prices down too far in order to survive, to the detriment of the others. He thought that a few large players in the industry was a far healthier way forward, so he set about achieving this. He began buying up all the competitors he could, offering the owners Standard Oil stock or cash, and making them partners in Standard Oil.

John D. Rockefeller ... on opportunity

I always tried to turn every disaster into an opportunity.

This expansion programme was conducted in great secrecy, one of Rockefeller's trademarks. He used to use code words to mean such things as 'buy' or 'sell' when corresponding with his senior executives, especially by telegram. But it wasn't long before it became apparent how enormous Standard Oil had become. To Rockefeller, this was the logical way for the industry to function – with him at the head of it of course. But Standard Oil was wielding ever greater power. It was forcing the railroads to pay it a levy on every barrel of oil shipped by any of its competitors. And by 1879 Standard Oil was doing about 90 per cent of the oil refining in the US.

Rockefeller was effectively in charge of the Standard Oil Trust – a cartel of ostensibly independent companies – despite the fact that he did not own a majority stake in it, thanks to having doled out shares so widely in his efforts to absorb other refiners. In this he was pioneering the future of big business; before Rockefeller, the leader of a large business organisation would always be the majority stakeholder.

As time passed, Standard Oil's aggressive marketing made it increasingly unpopular. With his typical attention to detail, Rockefeller wanted to force all grocery and hardware stores to sell only Standard kerosene and lubricants. Eventually, in 1892, the Trust was forced to break up into its component companies by the Ohio courts on the grounds that it was operating a monopoly. In fact, however, the dissolution had little practical effect since the same people were running all the companies concerned. Finally, in 1911, Standard Oil was forced to split into competitive companies.

By that time, Rockefeller had long since retired. He had suffered a mild nervous breakdown due to overwork in 1891–2, during which he lost all his hair. In 1897, at the age of 58, he had retired, and devoted the rest of his life to spending his vast fortune on good causes, from helping found the University of Chicago to setting up the Rockefeller Foundation. He died at the age of 97, 40 years after retiring from the organisation that made him the world's first billionaire.

ANITA RODDICK
1942–
Organisation: *The Body Shop*

Key idea: *Socially responsible business*

'I want to work for a company that contributes to and is part of the community. I want something not just to invest in. I want something to believe in.'

A nita Roddick was a lone voice questioning the value of free trade at a time when everyone else was championing it. In fact, she has virtually made a career out of going a different way from everyone else. When she first launched her business on the principles of respecting nature, animals and people, she was generally seen as a flaky liberal left over from the 1960s. But it must have struck a chord with the customers, because it went on to grow into one of those huge businesses Roddick herself criticised. Her success gave her the chance to show how she believed it should be done.

Roddick was born in Littlehampton, on the south coast of England, in 1942, the daughter of Italian immigrants. This made her feel like something of an outsider; she has always felt at home outside the establishment ever since. She wanted to become an actress but her mother persuaded her to train as a teacher instead. However, neither became a career because she took an opportunity to spend time on a kibbutz in Israel and ended up working her way around the world instead. This brought her into contact with people from cultures all around the globe, many of them pre-industrial, and gave her an understanding of how the rest of the world functions.

On her return, she met and married Gordon Roddick. They opened a restaurant in Littlehampton, and then a hotel. In 1976, Gordon Roddick set off to fulfil his dream of riding a horse all the way from Buenos Aires to New York. This left Anita Roddick at home with two children to support. She needed to find an income. She had £12,000 to

Anita Roddick ... on progress

We need to measure progress by human development, not gross product.

invest in a business, so she decided to open a shop in Brighton selling home-made shampoos and beauty creams in environmentally friendly packaging. She had learned all sorts of unusual ways to cleanse and refresh the body from her travels, and she researched further into the practices of the Amazons, Polynesians and others.

Roddick knew nothing about running a business, and the only business tenet she had to rely on was her husband's advice before he left to take sales of £300 a week. But she learnt that, 'Business was not a financial science, it's about trading: buying and selling. It's about creating a product or service so good that people will pay for it.' And they were certainly willing. Roddick had an initial burst of publicity due to the fact that she called her new store the Body Shop, and it was located next door to a funeral parlour. But it was more than that. Her products were terrific, and her timing was perfect. The 'green' movement was just beginning to take off and she was swept along on the bandwagon. She had even chosen the perfect colour for her shop – she had painted it green to cover the mould on the walls.

Roddick maintains that much of the thinking behind the recyclable, environmentally friendly packaging was inspired by her mother. Roddick's mother had lived through the war, when everything had to be re-used, and she continued her frugal methods after the war ended. It was this that made Roddick question modern retail practices. As she said, 'Why waste a container when you can refill it? And why buy more of something than you can use?'

Within six months, she had opened a second shop, and her husband had returned from his travels. He had the idea of franchising Body Shop stores, which enabled the company to self-finance its growth. Roddick did not charge franchise fees, but made her profits from wholesaling the products. These products are largely made by villagers from third world countries, according to Roddick's principles of 'Trade not Aid'. These villagers earn their living extracting nut oils, weaving plant fibres and so on to supply the Body Shop.

The Body Shop as an organisation is guided by Roddick's own personal values, and is closely associated with social responsibility, human rights issues, the environment and animal protection. It has helped

Anita Roddick ... on success

First, you have to have fun. Second, you have to put love where your labour is. Third, you have to go in the opposite direction to everyone else.

spearhead a number of campaigns over the years, beginning with the Save the Whale campaign in 1986, for which it worked closely with Greenpeace. The organisation's mission statement begins: 'To dedicate our business to the pursuit of social and environmental change.' At times, Roddick has been accused of operating business practices out of line with her professed principles, but she has always overcome such accusations, usually looking cleaner than before. She successfully sued a television company for libel in 1992 when it falsely attacked her over animal testing.

Looking after employees is also at the forefront of Roddick's priorities, which she sees as an extension of her belief in respect for people. In 1994, the Body Shop offered paternity leave to all its male employees. Roddick puts great effort into employee satisfaction, and has said, 'Our people are my first line of customers.'

The franchising of the business was so successful that by 1994, Roddick found herself heading up a huge organisation with hundreds of stores all around the world. But she felt the company was stagnating, and that it was time to bring in a professional management team. So much effort had gone into environmental issues that the core business wasn't getting the focused attention it needed. But Roddick wasn't entirely happy with the results, although she acknowledged the need for it. The increase in the product range that followed, and the logistical demands of distributing them all, inevitably led to a lot of red tape. And the organisation's structure had to change to accommodate it. Roddick said, 'We're having to grow up. We have to get methods and processes in, and the result of that is a hierarchy that comes in, and I think it's antiproductive.'

In 1998, Roddick finally stepped down as CEO of the Body Shop, and joined her husband as co-chairman. Her organisation now has nearly 2000 stores in almost 50 countries. Although her role in the direct running of the business is less active, she herself continues to work for the causes she believes in, both through her business and independently of it. Her organisation and her life have been so intimately bound up in her beliefs that she is permanently engrossed in her vision to bring higher moral values to the world of big business.

ALAN SAINSBURY

1902–1998

Organisation: *Sainsbury*

Key idea: *The British supermarket*

'It has always struck me as socially unjustifiable and economically unsound that a customer who gets credit, home delivery, plus personal service should pay the same price as a customer who goes into a shop, pays cash on the nail and takes the particular article away with her.'

Before Alan Sainsbury changed everything, shopping involved queuing until the shopkeeper was free to serve you, and then telling them what you wanted while they selected it for you. Then you went to the next shop and did the same thing. But when Sainsbury and his younger brother took over a thriving family business, they turned it into a pioneering enterprise which led the way in transforming British shopping habits.

J Sainsbury's was a family-run grocery business that began with just one shop in London. It had been founded in 1869 by Sainsbury's grandparents, who expanded the chain until by 1903 they had a hundred branches. When they retired, the business was taken over by Alan Sainsbury's father. After a private education, Sainsbury joined the family business in 1921 and worked behind the counter. Seventeen years later, his father retired leaving his two sons to run the business. Although he remained as chairman, he never interfered with his children's decisions.

Alan Sainsbury and his younger brother, Robert, developed an excellent working relationship. They shared responsibility for the business, Alan focusing on marketing and sales and Robert looking after finance and administration. They tended to agree on most important matters, but in any case the arrangement was that each had the final say in their own area of responsibility.

It wasn't long before the business was forced to adapt to World War II. The Sainsbury brothers were very aware of the social responsibility they had in a time of crisis, and their advertising reflected this with information about rationing, and a scheme of 'fair shares' for unrationed goods. Although Sainsbury was very involved in the business during the war, much of his time was also taken up as chief representative for the grocery industry on the retail advisory committees set up by the Ministry of Food.

But the war was bad for Sainsbury's. The chain had had an excellent reputation for quality and low prices which had drawn customers from quite a wide catchment area to each of its stores. But with rationing, housewives had to register with a local grocer, and travel to and from Sainsbury's stores became a luxury most couldn't afford. Not only that, but new controls restricted arrangements with many of their suppliers.

By the end of the war, people had changed their eating and buying habits. Sainsbury's now had access to a plentiful supply of fresh foods – agriculture had become highly mechanised and efficient as a result of the war – but people had grown used to buying canned and packet foods as an alternative to fresh, and these occupied most of Sainsbury's warehouse space. What the business needed to do was to increase throughput massively to maximise turnover, and to allow it to expand its product range.

But Sainsbury had a problem. He tried to expand the size of stores, but the shop counter simply created a bottleneck. There was a limit to how many customers you could serve in a day, and it wasn't a high enough one.

While Sainsbury was puzzling over this problem, the British government asked him and his brother to conduct a research trip to America to study US food retailing, in particular innovations in frozen food. But when they got there, they were far more interested in the burgeoning self-service food industry. What had happened in America was that the Depression had forced warehouses to cut down on distribution costs by introducing a form of self-service. This had developed into supermarkets where the customers helped themselves.

The idea was revolutionary to a British market. After all, the only system was that you asked the shop assistant for what you wanted and they fetched it for you. But Sainsbury could see that self-service was the answer to his problems. In early 1950, the brothers opened their first self-service store. They chose a branch in Croydon, which was a double store so they could convert one half of it and leave the other as before, and then compare the two.

Alan Sainsbury ... on change

My brother and I accepted the fact that the third generation could not and would not wish to run the business the same way as the second. The same way will no doubt apply to the fourth.

On the day the store opened, both brothers were at the door to greet shoppers and to hand them shopping baskets. The system was completely new to the people of Croydon, and it had to be carefully explained to them. One woman, being told that she had to carry her shopping around the store in the basket herself, threw the basket straight back at Sainsbury. But most people, once they'd got the idea, were very receptive to this more efficient, faster method of shopping. And Sainsbury had planned the layout of the store in meticulous detail to make it as customer-friendly as possible.

Sainsbury's father, meanwhile, knew what his sons were up to and was horrified. He didn't like to interfere with their management of the business but at the first opportunity he rushed over to Croydon. He watched the shop in operation, and then cross-examined his sons. By the end of the meeting he was converted entirely, and wanted every Sainsbury's store to go self-service immediately.

But it wasn't possible. Sainsbury had rather assumed, along with everyone else, that rationing was about to end. But the Korean War started the day before the Croydon store opened, and rationing didn't finally stop for another four years. Building licences were hard to get too so by 1954, when the rationing really did stop at last, Sainsbury had still managed to open only four self-service shops.

Mind you, those four extra years of waiting had given Sainsbury a chance to learn about self-service. When he and his brother had launched the new system they didn't know exactly what effect it would have on labour costs, turnover or profitability. They learnt a lot between 1950 and 1954, and when they started to roll out the new self-service system across the organisation, they had honed it to be highly effective for both the organisation and the customers.

Sainsbury was determined that the new supermarkets should offer the lowest prices possible, so he cut costs by abandoning Sainsbury's delivery service, and by abolishing credit facilities. The business had always looked after its employees, and now they introduced a five day working week in order to create conditions comparable with those in industry. But Monday was still traditionally washing day in British house-

> **Alan Sainsbury ... on on his competitors' view that the British public wouldn't take to self-service**
>
> How wrong they were. How lucky we were that they were wrong!

holds, and therefore demand at stores was much lower. So Sainsbury decided to close on Mondays and open on Saturdays, as well as staying open on local early-closing days and on Friday evenings.

Sainsbury's went from strength to strength, and Alan Sainsbury continued to innovate. He introduced new lines such as the hugely successful oven-ready frozen chickens, and he dreamt up the slogan 'Good Food Costs Less at Sainsbury's', which is still used today.

In 1967 Alan Sainsbury, who was later created Lord Sainsbury, retired as head of trading to become president of Sainsbury's, much as his father had done before him, leaving the next generation – including his three sons – in charge of the business. The family business had become one of the leading supermarket chains in Britain as a result of Sainsbury's visionary realisation that self-service was the answer to his problems. He started a trend in the UK which now dominates our shopping habits, and has seen Sainsbury's itself grow to over 400 stores and a group turnover of nearly £17.5 billion a year.

MARJORIE SCARDINO

1946–

Organisation: *Pearson*

Key idea: *Focus on the core business*

'I do my best in an atmosphere of energy, some urgency, and a good amount of humour.'

T he first woman to head a FTSE 100 company, Marjorie Scardino learned about business failure before she achieved major success. Her feisty approach to business hit the headlines when she took over the reins at Pearson plc – a slightly stodgy, trundling organisation – and streamlined the business more effectively than most people believed possible.

Scardino grew up in Texas. She trained as a lawyer and then went into journalism in 1970, where she soon became a desk editor. This was where she met her husband, a reporter named Albert Scardino. In 1978, the two of them decided to start a different kind of newspaper, and they moved to Savannah, Georgia to launch the *Georgia Gazette*. Since there was no guarantee they would make money, Marjorie Scardino became a partner in a local law firm as well as publishing the newspaper. It was a weekly paper which set out to expose corruption in high places, and it was a huge journalistic success. It played a part in putting 35 public officials behind bars and, in 1984, Albert's editorials won him a Pulitzer Prize.

But the *Georgia Gazette*'s financial achievements did not live up to the same standards; in fact it never earned a cent in profits, and in 1985 it folded. The Scardinos were left owing $250,000 – a sum it took them over ten years to pay off. Disheartened, they decided to move to New York to find work. Marjorie's luck – helped along considerably by her dynamic personality – improved and she was recommended by a headhunter for the job of number two to the new CEO of *The Economist*'s

> **Marjorie Scardino … on failure**
>
> Once you fail at something, you learn that you don't die.

US operations. However, the incoming CEO decided not to take the job after all, and recommended they appoint Scardino instead.

Her chief qualification was that she had run a failed weekly local newspaper and yet somehow she persuaded *The Economist*'s top people that you learn most from mistakes, and that she could handle the job. They took the gamble.

Scardino spent the next seven years running the US *Economist* operation. She adopted the strategy of identifying clearly the magazine's target readers, and then wasting no energy in going after them. She used direct mail, she handed out free copies at key shuttle terminals, and advertised in airports and train stations – anywhere she could catch the eye of travelling business people. Her approach paid off handsomely: the magazine's circulation in the US more than doubled. And she got herself noticed by her bosses in London, too.

In 1992, when *The Economist* wanted to find an international CEO to work from its headquarters in London, they turned to Scardino. She grabbed the opportunity and moved to London, where her husband decided to stay at home and look after the kids and write books, while she developed her career.

In her usual style, Scardino swept into *The Economist* and applied her clear, focused approach. In four years, the magazine's circulation had risen by over 100,000 and turnover had increased by 130 per cent. Scardino insisted the credit went to her deputies, saying 'I just send flowers and get out of the way.'

In 1996, Scardino was offered her greatest challenge yet: Pearson plc needed a new CEO. The huge media conglomerate, which owned businesses as diverse as Pearson TV, the Penguin Group, the *Financial Times* and Madame Tussaud's waxworks museum, was not performing as well as it should, and was in need of an overhaul. So instead of following its traditional, slightly fusty, pinstripe British traditions, Pearson decided to bring in an ousider – an American woman who had never run a public company before, but who had a reputation for shaking up a business and knocking it into shape.

Scardino took up the job on 1 January 1997. She set out her vision for Pearson when she got the job, saying 'Clearly, my responsibility is to ensure we make investors a return on their investments. I also be-

> ## Marjorie Scardino ... on a sense of purpose
>
> I think that the best companies are companies that have a real pur-
> pose, that offer their employees a chance to feel that when they get
> up in the morning, they really are making a difference in somebody's
> life.

lieve corporations have responsibilities to their employees, to make sure
they have stimulating jobs. Corporations also have the responsibility to
spend time on the community and on charity.'

From the off, Scardino brought her fast, energetic style of focused
management to her new job. Analysts had been eying up Pearson and
wondering about its breakup value. But Scardino pre-empted them by
breaking up the organisation herself in effect. Her strategy was to focus
Pearson on media and education, and to get rid of everything else. So
she sold off all its other interests, such as Madame Tussauds and Pearson's stake in Lazard investment banks. In other words, she turned a
disparate conglomerate into an organisation of closely related businesses. In her first couple of years, she sold off $3.2 billion of assets. But she
wasn't simply reducing and focusing operations.

Scardino was simultaneously buying up more than she was selling,
but all of it in Pearson's core field of media and education, strengthen-
ing an already powerful portfolio. In the same couple of years, she spent
over $5 billion on media and publishing acquisitions. And she invested
heavily in expanding Pearson's flagship publication, the *Financial Times*,
into the US, adopting the same strategy she had with *The Economist* of
identifying the target market clearly and then going after it relentlessly.
Once again, the strategy worked, and US sales of the *FT* rose by well
over 100,000 in her first three years at Pearson. The German edition she
launched was a big success, too.

To date, Scardino's success at Pearson has been huge. One Pearson executive described her as a person who 'says whatever she feels or
thinks, has no time for corporate politics, is energetic and full of bright
ideas which come in the shower at 2am and which have to be communi-
cated immediately.' She has been lauded for her clear, focused strategy,
which has turned Pearson back into a major player.

Much of her focus now has been turned to education – an area
where she feels Pearson can make a useful contribution, as well as profit
for itself – and the Internet. Pursuing both these aims, she has made
several deals with AOL, for example providing educational content and

services for some of AOL's online programmes. In 1999, Scardino became a non-executive director of AOL, whose chairman and CEO Steve Case described her as a 'visionary leader'.

CHARLES R. SCHWAB

1937–

Organisation: *The Charles Schwab Corporation*

Key idea: *Discount brokerage services*

'I knew from the start I would be an entrepreneur; my instincts for it were almost hard-wired.'

T ime was, the whole idea of buying and selling on the stock market was near impossible for the amateur. Quite apart from the cost of brokerage services, there was little or no information on which to base decisions. You wouldn't know where to start. But that was before Charles R. Schwab came along and made stock market trading affordable and accessible to the masses.

Schwab decided as a child that he wanted to make money. He started by selling walnuts, back in the 1940s, collecting them, bagging them up and selling them for $5 a sack. His enterprise did well on a modest scale, and he learnt a few of the basics of business. For example, 'If I wanted to make more money, I had to sell more walnuts.'

At the age of 12, he graduated to selling eggs door-to-door. He soon had a couple of dozen chickens, and he learnt about integrating his operation: he killed and plucked the old birds to sell, and he sold chicken fertiliser. Now he even had a couple of friends to help, with whom he shared the profits. Fledgling employees, you might say.

After a couple of years, Schwab decided there must be easier ways to earn money. So he sold off his egg business assets, and started caddying at the local golf club. By the time he went to Stanford University to study economics he was taking all sorts of holiday jobs. He tried selling door-to-door but found that selling wasn't his forté, and then he started working as a bank teller. Still an undergraduate, he finally found his niche: investing in the stock market.

Charles R. Schwab ... on integrating IT

Gone are the days when a company could afford to rope off its IT staff from the rest of the company. IT must be integrated and embedded into the centre of the company.

After earning his degree, followed by an MBA, Schwab went to work as a stockbroker. And in 1971 he set up his own business, The Charles Schwab Corporation. To begin with, this was a traditional brokerage except that Schwab wanted to run it ethically, with no pressure on investors, and he wanted to listen to his customers and let them determine the direction of the business.

By 1974, the company had become a discount brokerage, offering low prices and a fast ordering system. His pioneering ideas of avoiding high-pressure sales, together with the price incentive, soon made his company the largest discount broker in the US. In the 1980s, mutual funds became the most popular convenience investments for individuals looking for a diversified portfolio, and Schwab launched the Schwab Mutual Fund MarketPlace, offering a choice of hundreds of funds.

The company was booming, despite several upheavals, and in the late 1980s it went public. But perhaps its greatest success was its innovative move onto the Internet in 1995. Schwab was the first to see – perhaps inspired by his own personal passion for playing the stock market – that the Internet was made for individual investors. He was also influenced by noticing the fact that in 1994, for the first time, Americans bought more computers than television sets. He invested heavily in his Internet operations, and launched e.Schwab ahead of any of the competition, with a brilliantly easy-to-navigate, no-frills site which is fast and accurate and packed with information and objective guidance. In 1996, Schwab had 600,000 online accounts. By 1998 that figure had risen to 2.2 million. The Schwab Website has won awards for customer confidence and on-site resources.

Schwab's online brokerage is now the world's largest e-commerce site, handling as many as 300,000 trades a day, way ahead of the competition. But Schwab has continued to expand his bricks and mortar branches – 400 of them – where 70 per cent of new accounts are still opened. Schwab has around 7.5 million active investors, who between them hold assets of well in excess of $950 billion in their accounts.

Schwab has succeeded through being one step ahead of the competition, always ready with the next idea – from discount brokerage to ex-

Charles R. Schwab ... on customer satisfaction

Our vision is to be the most ethical and useful financial services firm ... Everything we do starts with the question 'Is this useful to the customer?' We don't start out with, 'Can we make money at it?' That part comes later.

ploiting the Internet. But his style of management is regarded as inspirational within the organisation too. Brokerage is a traditionally male-dominated industry, but Schwab – along with his co-CEO David S. Pottruck – have made sure they promote diversity at work. In consequence, 38 per cent of the 20,000-strong workforce are women, including 28 per cent of senior managers.

Schwab has always believed in progressive principles and in equality of respect for fellow workers. He has made sure his company reflects his own views, and has set up several programmes to promote diversity and employee benefits. The company has its own pregnancy support programme, return to work programme for new mothers, and paternity leave arrangements. It also helps employees who have elderly dependents, and supports flexible working.

Schwab's ten investing principles

Schwab considers it vital to give all investors objective advice, and he has devised ten investing principles which all his employees who deal with customers are taught to remember and pass on:

1 Start with the basics (this includes setting aside at least two to six months' living expenses in case of emergencies).
2 Get started now.
3 Know yourself (your own emotions, risk tolerance and so on will influence the most appropriate types of investments).
4 Invest for growth.
5 Take a long-term view.
6 Build a diversified portfolio.
7 Consider bonds and cash for diversification and income.
8 Minimise expenses.
9 Stay on track.
10 Be a lifelong investor.

Organisation: *General Motors*

Key idea: *The divisionalised corporation*

'My concept of the management scheme of a great industrial organi-sation, simply expressed, is to divide it into as many parts as consist-ently can be done, place in charge of each part the most capable ex-ecutive that can be found, and develop a system of co-ordination so that each part may strengthen and support each other part.'

A lfred Sloan is recognised as one of the greatest organisational geniuses in history, possibly the very greatest; an engineer who engineered an entire corporation rather than simply the cars it produced. Not only did he rescue General Motors from disaster and turn it into the biggest car manufacturer in the world, but he created a system of organisation which countless other corporations then used to pull themselves forwards. His principles have been preached by such business gurus as Peter Drucker and Jack Welch, and Sloan himself has won numerous accolades, including being one of the top four *Fortune* businessmen of the 20th century (alongside Henry Ford, Bill Gates and Thomas Watson Jr).

Sloan was born into a wealthy family in Brooklyn, where he showed promise from the start. He was a keen student, and trained in engineering at the Massachusetts Institute of Technology. He completed the course in only three years, graduating early, and then joined a failing roller bearing company in New Jersey. It hardly seemed like a promising career start, but before long Sloan bought the company, with help from his father, and turned it into a success by finding ways to sell roller bearings into the automobile industry. One of his customers was Henry Ford, whom Sloan would later do battle with in the competition to sell cars to America.

The company cost Sloan and his father $5000 in 1898. In 1916 they sold it for $13.5 million to William Durant, who incorporated it into his company General Motors. This made Sloan extremely rich (he took his share in GM stock), and it also made him a vice president of GM.

But GM was not a well-managed organisation. It was a bunch of unconnected businesses – Cadillac, Chevrolet, Buick and others – with mounting debts, which eventually became so bad that Durant was forced out and, in 1923, Sloan became president. His task was to save the business and make it profitable again.

Sloan found he had a disparate group of entirely separate businesses to run. Each decided what cars it should make and what price it should charge for them, and each business had its own bank account, which made it difficult for the central administration to wrest any financial control from them. At the time, Ford had 60 per cent of the auto market with his popular Model T, and the current wisdom was that the only room for growth was in the luxury car market.

Sloan disagreed. He could see that the luxury market would never be that big, and he determined to play Ford at his own game. With a range of cars as broad as Sloan had under the GM umbrella, he determined to manufacture a car 'for every purse and every purpose'. That would require some kind of co-operation between each of the GM companies, so that each was positioned differently in the market. And that required centralised policies.

Sloan set about reorganising the business completely, and in the process he created a blueprint for organising large corporations everywhere. He partly used the US Constitution as a model, in which the states – or corporate divisions – were allowed to operate independently, but had to follow policies set out by committees (federal laws).

His first move was to set up a central administration which allocated resources and co-ordinated all eight of the operating divisions (or strategic business units, as they would be called today). Each division had to liaise with this corporate office to get whatever it needed in the way of factories, money, staff and so on. Sloan also laid out procedures across the organisation for recruiting, reporting, budgeting and so on. And he set up interdivisional councils where managers could discuss ways to exploit economies of scale or to share ideas.

However, it was central to Sloan's system that in all other ways the operating divisions should remain autonomous, as they had been under Durant. Indeed he even insisted that divisions stop selling each other components at cost, since this made it impossible to judge their true profitability. Each division was allowed to remain under its own sovereignty.

> ## Alfred P. Sloan ... on recognising potential
>
> It is impossible to get the measure of what an individual can accomplish unless the responsibility is given him.

The function of the central office was to set policy. But Sloan believed that policy must come from the people who work with it, so he instituted a system to make this work. He created an Executive Committee, made up of people from the central office, which was there to form policies. And he also formed an Operations Committee, which comprised the Executive Committee plus all the General Managers of the operating divisions. The Operations Committee discussed what policies might be needed, tested policy proposals, and ensured that the two groups met regularly and listened to each other's ideas. As far as Sloan was concerned, you couldn't set policies without the people who put them into practice.

This approach had another benefit for Sloan and GM. As the divisional managers got used to meeting each other week after week, alongside the executive, they gradually came to see themselves as part of the larger organisation, and recognised that what was good for GM was good for them. They were no longer tempted to compete with each other, and they co-operated with the centralisation of policy.

Sloan was clear that, while GM was one big organisation with centralised policy-making, each division really was autonomous. As he explained: 'Even when we make recommendations from the general corporation's office, the head of a division is at liberty to accept or reject – and once in a while he rejects.

'At first many of our men believed that this was too good to be true. Some feared that although we meant it, we could not carry it out. They began tentatively unleashing their brains and making important decisions, but they kept one eye on the general corporation office, expecting at any moment to receive a veto of their decisions, or an order that would conflict with their decisions.

'No such thing happened. We do not issue orders. I have never issued an order since I have been the operating head of this corporation.'

The effect of Sloan's reorganisation and repositioning was that by 1925, GM had overtaken Ford as the biggest car manufacturer, and has maintained its position at the top of the table ever since. By 1940, Ford's share of the US market had dropped to 18.9 per cent, while GM's share had risen to 47.5 per cent.

Alfred P. Sloan ... on policy making

Where do policies come from, if they are to be useful in the business? Out of the business itself. And that is where our policies come from. They must come from the men who are in daily contact with problems. They must handle activities of whatever sort, whether production, sales, service or finance. Policies are not correct which do not fit such conditions. Our policies come from the bottom. Everything possible in the organisation starts from the bottom.

Sloan remained at the helm of GM until 1956, and managed to steer the organisation successfully for his entire period of leadership. The only blemish on his record was his refusal, like Ford, to deal with the unions. After the strikes of 1937 – and government intervention – he was finally forced to recognise the union. In other ways, however, Sloan regarded the development of his people with an importance not often attached to HR in the first half of the 20th century. And although he occasionally missed policy meetings, he never missed a personnel meeting.

After his retirement (he remained a member of the board until his death in 1966), Sloan wrote his seminal management book, *My Years at General Motors.* His methods, which it explains, have been adopted by numerous organisations. But it isn't as simple as it looks, and Sloan turned out to have been a master of the balancing act between decentralisation and central control. GM itself floundered later on when the system grew more complex, and too many committees and reporting structures sprang up. Without Sloan's light touch at the helm, the bureaucracy became overpowering.

Sloan himself had warned of the dangers: 'In practically all our activities we seem to suffer from the inertia resulting from our great size. There are so many people involved and it requires such a tremendous effort to put something new into effect that a new idea is likely to be considered insignificant in comparison with the effort that it takes to put it across ... Sometimes I am almost forced to the conclusion that General Motors is so large and its inertia so great that it is impossible for us to be leaders.'

ALAN SUGAR
1947–

Organisation: *Amstrad*

Key idea: *Cheap home electronics*

'I think if you went out into the street and stopped ten people and said "Amstrad", they would say "oh yeah, computers, satellite, good value for money, always coming up with something new".'

One of Britain's most famous barrow-boy-turned-business-men, Alan Sugar has headed up Amstrad for over 30 years, despite recurrent predictions of its imminent collapse. Despite three decades experience of big business, he still retains his instinctive mistrust – even contempt – for the City, for consultants, for most of the trappings of industry.

Alan Sugar founded his company, Amstrad (an acronym derived from Alan M Sugar Trading), when he was only 19, trading in electrical goods from the back of a van. In 1970 he began manufacturing goods, operating on the simple principle that if you could make the goods cheaper, more people would buy them. Sugar made them cheaper by injection-moulding plastic turntable covers while the competition was using more expensive production methods.

Sugar continued to expand his company, selling radios, televisions, audio amplifiers and the like at the low end of the market. Then in 1984, he decided to go into the home PC market, despite the fact that it didn't yet exist. There were PCs – dominated by IBM – in large businesses, and they were selling with high profit margins. The few home PCs around were simply used for playing games. This was the market Sugar decided to go into, and he launched the first mass market Home Computer package, taking a large chunk of the market from Commodore and Sinclair.

But Sugar wasn't stopping there. Despite media scepticism he was convinced that it wouldn't be long before small offices had PCs, and

---

Alan Sugar ... on the Amstrad culture

At Amstrad the staff start early and finish late. Nobody takes lunches – they may get a sandwich slung on their desk – there's no small talk. It's all action and the atmosphere is amazing, and the *esprit de corps* is terrific. Working hard is fun.

---

homeowners would want them too. So Amstrad began to design a dedicated word processor.

It was launched in 1985 and, true to Sugar's strategy of keeping the costs right down, it retailed for only £399. That included the operating software and a dot matrix printer. Sugar embarked on a typically blunt advertising campaign, including one ad that depicted a truck dumping a load of typewriters at a tip. The PCW 8256 (as it was called) was an instant hit, and Amstrad sold over 350,000 in the first eight months.

Sugar's next shot across the bows of the computer giants was a mass market IBM-compatible PC, which he managed to sell for only a quarter the price of its nearest competitors, giving Amstrad 25 per cent of the European PC market by the end of 1986. In 1989, Sugar launched his next low price innovation, the first combined fax, phone and answering machine. It gave him over half the personal fax market.

But the seeds of Amstrad's downfall were in its success. The low price products it pioneered hugely speeded up the acceptance of the PC in small businesses and homes. But other PC manufacturers began importing cheaply from the Far East so that they could have a share in this booming low price market. And Sugar was squeezed by the competition he had just stolen a march on. Amstrad eventually had to pull out of the PC manufacturing market where Sugar had made his name, and diversify into other areas such as satellite TV and phone technology.

Despite frequent setbacks, Sugar has kept Amstrad going. And he is still innovating with products that often meet with scepticism but which perform more often than not. In fact, Sugar almost takes pride in proving the analysts and the media wrong as often as possible. He doesn't care what they think; his focus is clearly on the mass market, 'the truck driver and his wife' who Sugar designs his products for.

He is scathing about university-educated types who think they know what is good for a company. Back in 1993, when Amstrad was starting to flounder as the competition brought their prices down to meet theirs, Sugar was persuaded to call in a team of consultants. They persuaded him to become chairman and to appoint a chief executive

---

Alan Sugar ... on looking ahead

Anyone who talks five-year plans talks crap.

---

to look after the day-to-day business, and they began restructuring the company into business units. But Sugar hated all the consultants' jargon, and finally snapped when he encountered an experienced Amstrad engineer being told what to do by a young consultant. His response was to get rid off all the consultants, and the new chief executive too, and reclaim control of the business.

Sugar is, crucially, his own 'man in the street', and he has a healthily common-sense attitude to much of the new technology around today. He believes that much of the current market for hi-tech equipment has been exaggerated by the affluent and by the technofreaks. 'But,' he argues, 'they don't keep us going. What keeps us going is the mass market.' For this reason he is heretically suspicious of WAP mobile phones. He doesn't see a real market for a small phone with a small screen so there's not much you can read on it: 'Why would Mr Average have a WAP? For paying his electric bill? Why does he have to be out in the street to do it? He can do that at home. We need a bit of coming down to earth.'

Lately, Amstrad's share value has slumped, but Sugar (now Sir Alan Sugar) remains confident as always that it is only a matter of time before it picks up. And if his past form – and his understanding of the mass market – is anything to go by, it'll be a long time before anyone dares write off Alan Sugar and Amstrad.

Key idea: *Take care of your employees, and they'll take care of the customers*

'There is only one boss. The customer. And he can fire everybody in the company from the chairman on down, simply by spending his money somewhere else.'

S am Walton was a hugely charismatic leader who started out as a small-time department store owner and built up his chain of discount stores until it became the world's biggest retail chain. His philosophy was to look after his employees so well that they were deeply motivated and loyal. Alongside this, he really believed in putting the customer first.

Sam Walton was already in his 40s, and operating a successful chain of around 15 traditional department stores in Arkansas, Missouri and Oklahoma, when he had the idea that sparked the Wal-Mart revolution. A local barber in Arkansas began opening discount stores outside towns where Walton had his stores. And Walton had the vision to see that this was where retailing was headed.

In 1962, the very first Wal-Mart store opened in Rogers, Arkansas. Walton was determined to drive prices down as far as he could by cutting costs, by going straight to producers and bypassing the middleman, and by cutting his own profit margins. This was the same year that the discount chains KMart, Woolco and Target were launched, but no one noticed a small-town outfit like Wal-Mart.

Sam Walton's approach was simple: drop the price and sell more units. According to Walton: 'By cutting your price, you can boost your sales to a point where you earn far more at the cheaper retail than you would have by selling the item at the higher price. In retailer language, you can lower your markup but earn more because of the increased volume.'

With such narrow profit margins, Sam Walton had no option but to expand his operation fast and open new stores. And while everyone else was catering for the big towns and cities, Walton concentrated on small-town America, which none of his competitors had seen any value in. He would fly his plane over groups of small towns, and locate a suitable intersection between them, never more than a day's drive from the nearest distribution centre, to keep costs down. Then he would land his plane on the spot, buy up a few fields and open another store.

Walton had a flair for anticipating the future. In 1966 he had twenty stores, and he recognised that he couldn't grow fast enough unless he computerised his operation. So he attended an IBM school in order to identify the smartest person in the class, whom he then hired to computerise Wal-Mart. He was so committed to efficient computerisation that Wal-Mart eventually became an acknowledged model of just-in-time stock control and complex computerised logistics. In fact, even today, the Pentagon is the only organisation with a larger computer database than Wal-Mart.

Sam Walton was a staunch believer in looking after people, both employees and customers. He advocated showing appreciation and giving praise to staff (whom he termed associates), listening to their views, creating a fun atmosphere for them to work in, and sharing profits with them. When Walton visited a factory in Korea where the workers had a company cheer, he was so impressed he brought the idea back to his own organisation. The cheer begins 'Give me a W!...' and ends 'Who's number one? The customer!'

Walton endeared himself to his hugely loyal staff through his charisma, his enthusiasm, and by treating each person as an individual and welcoming new ideas from them all. He travelled constantly, visiting every store as often as he could. And they loved his eccentricity, too. Despite being the richest man in America, he was careful with money, and insisted that cutting costs included keeping his own expenses down. So he stayed at budget hotels, wore clothes from his own Wal-Mart stores, worked out of a slightly run-down office, and drove around in a shabby pick-up truck (when he wasn't flying his plane from store to store). When questioned on his choice of vehicle, he would say 'What am I supposed to haul my dogs around in? A Rolls Royce?'

Wal-Mart was reaping the rewards of everyone else's failure to consider small-town America's potential for retailing. And still no one had really noticed Sam Walton. But all that changed in 1985, when Forbes

---

Sam Walton ... on staff loyalty

Our philosophy is that management's role is simply to get the right people in the right places to do a job and then encourage them to use their own inventiveness to accomplish the task at hand.

---

magazine announced that he was the richest man in the US, thanks to his 39 per cent holding in Wal-Mart.

Once Sam Walton became a public figure, attention focused on him and his chain of stores, which was now overtaking competitors such as KMart and Sears. The national press began to criticise him for ruining the countryside and changing the style of retailing for ever. But the public just didn't take the bait. They loved Sam Walton for his down-to-earth style – driving pick-up trucks rather than limos – for his charisma and, most of all, for giving them 'every day low prices'.

One of Walton's most famous, and popular, escapades came in 1983 when he lost a bet to his CEO, David Glass. He said afterwards that it was one of the few times he was publicly embarrassed. He had bet Glass that Wal-Mart couldn't make a rise in pre-tax profits of over eight per cent that year. If they did, he would dance the hula on Wall Street. In the event, the company recorded an increase of 8.04 per cent. Sam Walton duly turned up at Wall Street, in full hula costume, only to find that Glass had invited the national newspapers and network TV stations, who gave nationwide publicity to this somewhat unconventional behaviour from a company chairman. Walton was embarrassed but said, 'At Wal-Mart, when you make a bet like I did, you always pay up.'

The Wal-Mart culture of putting the customer first influences everything its people do. Among Walton's guiding principles are 'The Sundown Rule', which ensures that any problem or request is always resolved by the end of the same day; 'Exceeding Customer Expectations'; the 'Ten Foot Attitude', which stipulates that – in Sam Walton's words – 'whenever you come within ten feet of a customer, you will look him in the eye, greet him and ask him if you can help him'; and 'Every Day Low Prices', which includes passing on any savings to the customer.

Despite becoming the world's biggest retailer, employing well over half a million people in the US, Sam Walton always insisted that the chain's strength was in its local identity. So stores sell locally made goods, and every store employs 'people greeters' who welcome shoppers at the entrance. Each store gives a college scholarship to a local school leaver, and supports local charities (chosen by the associates).

Sam Walton ... on satisfying customers

If you take care of the people in the stores, they will take care of the customers in the same manner.

Much of Walton's success came from his determination to view Wal-Mart as a single, small-town store. He explained, 'If we ever get carried away with how important we are because we're a great big $50 billion chain – instead of one store in Blytheville, Arkansas, or Mc-Comb, Mississippi, or Oak Ridge, Tennessee – then you can probably close the book on us.'

Sam Walton died in 1992, the richest man ever in America at that time. But his philosophy continued to thrive at Wal-Mart, and its turn-over is now five times greater than it was then. Like any huge organisation Wal-Mart comes in for a great deal of stick from the press, especially without its larger-than-life figurehead any more. It is accused of squeezing out local traders, riding roughshod over legislation, and employing third world sweatshop labour. But thanks to Sam Walton's brand-building genius, small-town Americans still flood to his stores.

Sam Walton's 10 rules for success

Perhaps the best way to sum up Sam Walton's leadership principles is with his own top ten rules for success, which he published in his own book, *Sam Walton: Made in America, My Story* (Sam Walton, John Huey Bantam Books 1996).

1 Commit to your business.
2 Share your profits with all your associates.
3 Motivate your partners.
4 Communicate everything you possibly can to your partners.
5 Appreciate everything your associates do for the business.
6 Celebrate your success.
7 Listen to everyone in your company.
8 Exceed your customer's expectations.
9 Control your expenses better than your competition.
10 Swim upstream.

JACK WARNER
1892–1978

Organisation: *Warner Brothers*

Key idea: *Quality on a budget*

(To Einstein) 'I have a theory of relatives, too. Don't hire 'em.'

T he group of brothers who gave the world *The Jazz Singer* and *Casablanca* was a strange and uncomfortable mix of personalities. The strongest artistic influence, and the longest lasting owner of the company, was the youngest Warner brother of all: Jack.

There were 12 Warner children altogether, children of Polish Jewish immigrants who travelled widely around the US until 1903, when their father settled in Ohio where he opened a cobbler's shop, a butcher's shop and then a bicycle shop. In 1904, when Jack was just 12, his eldest brother Harry visited Pittsburgh and noticed how people were flocking to the movie theatres. He and brother number two, Sam, persuaded their father to raise the money for them to buy a projector. Sam had managed to get hold of a copy of *The Great Train Robbery*, and the entire family began touring the eastern States showing their movie. Eventually they found a nickelodeon in Pennsylvania where they could show their movie permanently, while Jack entertained the audience with his singing during the intermission.

In 1912, four of the Warner brothers – Harry, Sam, Albert and Jack – started to make their own movies. Most of these were shorts, and were not great successes. However, their luck turned in 1918 when they made a movie called *My Four Years in Germany*. It was their first hit, and it earned them enough money to buy up a ten-acre plot in Los Angeles to build their own studio, which they called Warner Bros.

Harry was the real businessman of the family, so he became company president, and ran its headquarters in New York. He was a serious-minded man, eldest of the brothers, who hoped that movies would be

---

Jack Warner's son ... on Warner's ego

If his brothers hadn't hired him, he'd have been out of work.

---

used mainly to educate people. Sam was the CEO, jovial and gregarious, he was always ready to try new ideas. It was he who pushed the studio into making the first ever commercially successful sound picture. Albert, placid and easygoing, was the treasurer and head of sales and distribution. And that left the youngest brother, Jack, running the Hollywood studio with Sam and in charge of production, directing most of the studio's early movies and dealing with the actors and writers.

Harry soon realised that the business was too dependent on the distributors to show their movies, so he bought up a key distributor and built up a chain of 500 theatres. Meanwhile, Jack was busy making a series of dramas, something no other studio had done before. He signed the actor John Barrymore on an exclusive contract, and Darryl Zanuck to write scripts for them.

Warner Brothers pioneered talking pictures, and their first big commercial sound success was *The Jazz Singer* starring Al Jolson, in which Jolson actually spoke a small amount of dialogue. It had been Sam's project, but he died suddenly the night before it opened. The following year, the remaining three brothers released the first complete sound film, *Lights of New York*. It was a massive success, grossing $2 million (having cost only $40,000).

Jack Warner kept the studio going through the depression by producing feature films, especially gangster movies, faster than any of the other studios – at a rate of about 100 a year. Cartoons were another of Warner's successes, with characters including Daffy Duck and Bugs Bunny, and the Looney Tunes series. Warner also produced Busby Berkeley's musical extravaganzas, and swashbuckling movies starring names such as Errol Flynn. By the 1940s he was turning out the likes of *The Maltese Falcon* and *Casablanca*.

Warner paid his stars – names such as Flynn, Bogart and Cagney – less than the competition was paying. He earned a reputation for tight budgeting, without apparently damaging the artistic value of his movies. He was a firm, often domineering studio boss, who frequently clashed with his stars and his writers – notably Bette Davis, Olivia de Havilland, Bogart and Cagney. When he earned an Oscar, Al Jolson complained, 'I can't see what Jack Warner can do with an Oscar. It can't

Jack Warner ... on retirement

You're nothing if you don't have a studio. Now I'm just another millionaire, and there are a lot of 'em around.

say yes.' Warner also, inevitably, clashed more and more with his older, more serious and idealistic brother, Harry.

Jack Warner could be overpowering, even cruel, but he was also known for his sense of humour. When told that Reagan had been elected governor of California he commented, 'It's our fault. We should have given him better parts.' On being introduced to Mme Chiang Kai-chek, he was heard quietly remarking that he had forgotten his laundry.

Jack Warner was the little brother who was constantly trying to prove that he was better than the rest of them. His ego was massive and it was only a matter of time before relations with his brothers soured. By the 1950s, Warner Brothers was suffering from the growth of television and the enforced sale of its movie theatres. Harry and Albert took the opportunity to get out, and sold their shares in 1956, leaving Jack Warner at last in sole charge of the organisation.

Although times were tough, Warner managed to keep the studio thriving, and had further successes such as *My Fair Lady* in 1964. He eventually retired in 1967, selling his interests in Warner Brothers, and became an independent producer. He missed the power and control of running a studio more than he missed making the movies.

Jack Warner died in 1978, and missed what would have been the huge satisfaction of seeing his company merge with Time Inc to form Time Warner Inc. Without his clear vision of what he wanted, his firm hand on the chequebook and his artistic talent, the studio probably wouldn't have survived to stamp his name on the world's biggest media corporation.

THOMAS J. WATSON JR

1914–1993

Organisation: *IBM*

Key idea: *Corporate values*

'If an organisation is to meet the challenges of a changing world, it must be prepared to change everything about itself except beliefs as it moves through corporate life … The only sacred cow in an organisation should be its basic philosophy of doing business.'

Thomas J. Watson was described by *Fortune* as 'arguably the greatest capitalist who ever lived'. He took over a hugely successful company from his father, who had founded it, and turned it into a massive operation at the forefront of the global technological revolution of the 1950s and 60s. Not only was he a visionary when it came to predicting the growth of computers, but he was also an innovative and influential management thinker. Under his leadership, IBM generated more wealth for its shareholders than any other company in business history, a record that stood until the 1990s.

Curiously enough, the young Watson Jr never expected to grow up to be anything much. He was convinced he could never step into the shoes of his formidable father, and could be reduced to tears at the prospect of having to go into the family business. Watson later said, 'The secret I learned early on from my father was to run scared and never think I had made it.'

Watson did poorly at school, and barely scraped through college, spending most of his time drinking and dancing rather than studying. After university he reluctantly joined the IBM sales school, although his enthusiasm was for flying aeroplanes and partying. However, Watson was saved, in a sense, by the war. He was a highly successful pilot, with nerves of steel, who flew on dangerous supply routes across Russia, India and China. The experience gave Watson the confidence he had lacked before.

After the war, Watson planned to become an airline pilot. But he had got to know the Army Air Forces' inspector general during the war, who expressed surprise at this ambition, saying he had always assumed Watson Jr would go back and run IBM. Watson was astounded and asked the general if he really thought he was up to the job. 'Of course,' replied the general.

So that's what he did. He spent the next ten years working alongside his father, each of them as irascible and as argumentative as the other. And there was plenty to argue about. Thomas Watson Senior had built up his company selling all sorts of equipment from meat slicing machines to weighing scales. But the business had gradually become focused on tabulating machines which processed information using punched cards. These machines were widely used to calculate hours worked and wages paid.

But Watson Jr saw that this machinery would soon become outmoded, and that the future lay in computers. The early vacuum-tube computers could already calculate ten times faster than IBM's machines. Watson's father, however, disagreed. He saw a limited market for computers, but couldn't imagine his tabulators ever becoming obsolete. Watson Jr had to fight his father to recruit electronics experts, double the R&D budget, and launch into the computer market ahead of giants such as Univac.

However, he managed to win enough of the battles and by the mid-50s, IBM's computers were a hot product. By the early 1960s, IBM was firmly established as the runaway leader in the computer market. In 1956, Thomas Watson Sr finally retired, just six weeks before his death, and at last his son had full control over the business. His sense of urgency drove IBM at high speed; this, Watson understood, was the key factor in staying ahead of such a fast-moving market: 'The worst possible thing we could do was to lie dead in the water with any problem. Solve it, solve it quickly, solve it right or wrong. If you solved it wrong, it would come back and slap you in the face, and then you could solve it right.'

In the early 1960s, Watson took the most massive gamble, with the kind of steely determination with which he had flown his wartime planes. He committed $5 billion – around three times IBM's revenue – to developing a new kind of computer. The System/360 was intended to be a range of mutually compatible computers which would enable customers to start small and upgrade as they needed to, keeping the same software as they did so. The gamble paid off. The System/360 was a massive success and revolutionised the industry, and IBM's revenue jumped to $7.5 billion by 1970, with a market value of $36 billion.

Thomas J. Watson Jr … on belief

Don't just put your heart into the business. Put the business into your heart.

But for all Watson's vision as a marketeer, he is remembered as much for his management style. He set out many of his principles in his book *A Business and Its Beliefs: The Ideas that Helped Build IBM*, published in 1963. Watson argued that the only things that must never change in a business are its core beliefs. In the case of IBM there were three: give full consideration to each individual employee, spend a lot of time making customers happy, and go the last mile to do things right. Watson strongly believed that a business would stand or fall by its beliefs, and that these should inform all its decisions, policies and actions. Any action or policy that violates the central beliefs of the organisation should be abandoned.

Certainly IBM's three core beliefs had been established under Thomas Watson Sr, and Watson Jr had adhered to these whilst completely changing the focus of the business from tabulators to computers, from a solid manufacturing company to a fast moving hi-tech industry. It was these beliefs which Watson used to drive the business, and which he used to create a corporate culture committed to serving customers whatever it took.

Watson looked after his rank-and-file employees and adopted a paternalistic attitude to them. Salary and perks were generous, and many employees bought or were given company stock. But with his managers he was tough, and the higher they climbed, the less forgiving he was with them. Watson's father had favoured yes men, but Watson Jr had the opposite approach: 'I never hesitated to promote someone I didn't like. The comfortable assistant – the nice guy you like to go fishing with – is a great pitfall. I looked for those sharp, scratchy, harsh, almost unpleasant guys who see and tell you about things as they really are.'

Watson had various techniques for handling his 'scratchy' managers, including what he called the penalty box: a short term but chastening transfer away from the fast track. Occasionally the transfer might last longer: Watson put his younger brother Dick in charge of the System/360 development programme and, when it began to fall behind schedule, he demoted him, ending his chances of reaching top management at IBM.

Thomas J. Watson Jr ... on people

I believe the real difference between success and failure in a corporation can very often be traced to the question of how well the organisation brings out the great energies and talents of its people. What does it do to help these people find common cause with each other?

Watson retired in 1971 following a heart attack, at the age of 57. As well as continuing to fly aeroplanes, he also served as US ambassador to Moscow. Unlike most successful business leaders, he had always had a life outside the organisation, and he continued to live it for over 20 years after he left IBM.

JACK WELCH
1935–

Organisation: *General Electric*

Key idea: *Be number 1 or 2 in your field ... or get out*

'We are betting everything on our people – powering them, giving them the resources, and getting out of their way.'

'N eutron Jack' Welch is one of the most extraordinary business phenomena of the last twenty years of the 20th century. He took over the tenth most valuable organisation in the world when everyone thought it was performing well, and showed how much better it could be done by making it the world's most valuable company. The whirlwind style of leadership he brought to GE has been emulated all over the world, though rarely with his mastery of it, and has helped to transform numerous other corporations.

Jack Welch was an altar boy at high school, and suffered from a stammer in childhood that he never fully overcame. He went to university in Massachusetts, and then in Illinois where he earned a PhD in chemical engineering. He joined General Electric as a junior engineer, but in 1961 he quit the company because he couldn't stand the bureaucracy. However, his boss talked him into taking the job back, and so he began to work his way up the organisation.

By 1973, Welch was a divisional vice president. When asked on his employee evaluation form to state his long-term goal he wrote that he aimed to become CEO. Eight years later, he achieved his aim. And General Electric didn't know what had hit it.

It's hard to know where to start describing Welch's achievements. But perhaps the best place is to start where he started. Welch took over GE when the world economy was in a pretty poor state, and GE's stock had done dreadfully, along with just about everyone else's – it had lost 50 per cent of its value in real terms over the previous ten years.

But to put this into context, *Fortune* magazine had just surveyed the CEOs of the *Fortune* 500. They voted GE the best-managed company among them, and Welch's predecessor, Reg Jones, the best CEO. But that didn't stop Welch launching what he called a revolution at GE.

Welch was one of the forward-thinking managers of his generation – though far from the only one – who saw that the world was changing. Manufacturing was on the wane and corporations were becoming bloated. Western businesses were being threatened by the new Japanese economy with its more streamlined style, and service and information would be the keywords of the next two decades. Many enlightened managers saw the problems, but Welch led the way in creating solutions.

He determined that GE would become the world's most valuable organisation, and such an ambitious aim meant cutting out all dead wood and refocusing the business. Welch announced that every GE business must be number 1 or number 2 in its industry, or it would have to go. He focused the business on service industries and junked any part of it that had no competitive advantage. This meant going into nearly 120 new businesses, and selling over 70.

Next, Welch set about reorganising the corporation and getting rid of the bureaucracy he so hated. One of his heroes was Alfred P. Sloan, and Welch got rid of large swathes of the corporate structure, devolving power to individual businesses. This meant virtually eliminating the corporate strategic planning department so that GE businesses could do their own planning. GE had spent years effectively squashing individuality in the organisation with endless rule books, procedures and guidance books. Welch trashed the lot, telling his managers to think for themselves. He warned them against bureaucracy and instructed them to 'Fight it. Hate it. Kick it. Break it.'

Welch wanted an informal company, an organisation without boundaries. He did away with whole layers of management, and encouraged departments and businesses to communicate and share ideas with each other, to 'knock down the walls that separate us from each other on the inside and from our key constituents on the outside.' As he put it later, after he had achieved his aim: 'Boundaryless behaviour is a way of life here. People really do take ideas from A to B. And if you take an idea and share it, you are rewarded. In the old culture, if you had an idea, you'd keep it. Sharing it with someone else would have been stupid, because the bureaucracy would have made him the hero, not you.'

Welch appeared to drive a hurricane through General Electric, forcing change at unstoppable speed. He himself, however, saw it differently, and expressed the barely credible regret later that he hadn't moved

Jack Welch ... on informality

The story about GE that hasn't been told is the value of an informal place. I think it's a big thought. I don't think people have ever figured out that being informal is a big deal.

even faster. His defence was that GE was such a valuable commodity already that he was 'afraid of breaking it'.

Welch was always a demanding manager from the start, forcing his managers to think for themselves and being prepared to argue loudly with them to make them do so. Meetings were followed up with a written summary from Welch of the commitments the manager has made. These were followed up again until they were met. You can't run an organisation the size of GE on the back of just one man's talent. Which is why Welch put huge effort into developing managerial talent. He demonstrated how it should be done, nurtured promising managers and gave them enough free rein to practise their skills. He says, 'The biggest accomplishment I've had is to find great people. An army of them. They are all better than most CEOs. They are big hitters, and they seem to thrive here.'

So are they really better than most CEOs? Well, many of them have gone on to become CEOs of other organisations. Welch has developed the talent that now runs such companies as Home Depot, 3M, Fiat SpA, Amazon.com and plenty more, all taking lessons from Welch's GE with them. It is a part of what makes his influence so wide-reaching.

Another of Welch's great cultural changes was his readiness to learn from other organisations. And not only learn from them, but give them credit for the ideas he took from them. GE was the classic corporation that didn't want to know about any idea that was 'not-invented-here': Welch put a stop to all that and loudly proclaimed that he had learnt organisation management from Alfred Sloan, or fast market intelligence from Wal-Mart.

In fact, most corporations today have learnt at least as much from Welch as from anyone else, and he is hailed as the greatest manager of his generation – even of the 20th century – by business media, gurus and organisations, and by CEOs around the world. And quite right too. Welch has created more shareholder value than any other business leader in the world, raising the market value of GE from $12 billion in 1981 to over $400 million today. And under his tenure GE has risen to compete only with Microsoft for the accolade of 'world's most valuable

Jack Welch ... on leadership

Good business leaders create a vision, articulate the vision, passionately own the vision, and relentlessly drive it to completion.

company', the two giants constantly jostling each other for position at the top of the tree.

At the end of December 2000, Jack Welch retired from GE, leaving as his legacy a streamlined, efficient corporation packed with talented people, voted America's Most Admired Company by *Fortune* in 2000. He took GE to the top, and kept it there for 20 years, by following his three prime principles:

Jack Welch's three operating principles

- Boundaryless ... in all our behaviour.
- Speed ... in everything we do.
- Stretch ... in every target we set.

ROBERT WOODRUFF

1889–1985

Organisation: *Coca-Cola*

Key idea: *The worldwide brand*

'There is no limit to what a man can do or how far he can go if he doesn't mind who gets the credit.'

R obert Woodruff seemed to go out of his way to avoid running Coca-Cola, but eventually landed up in the job somehow, and stayed there for sixty years. During that time he turned Coca-Cola into the world's most recognised brand, launched the six-pack, introduced soft drinks at filling stations, and even redesigned Father Christmas. It was Woodruff's mission to enable every thirsty person in the world to have a glass of Coca-Cola – a goal he almost achieved.

Robert Woodruff was the son of Ernest Woodruff, who was president of Coca-Cola. Young Woodruff was a poor student who dropped out of high school, but went to Georgia Military Academy where he organised everything from the school publication to the sports teams.

At his father's wish, Woodruff went to college, but was soon expelled for poor attendance. He started working as a labourer but was soon fired for no apparent reason. He got a job as a salesman, but was fired from that, too. In fact, he was fired from a whole series of jobs. Eventually, about to marry and in need of money, he accepted an offer of work from his father. After some success Woodruff was in line for a pay rise, but it was vetoed by his father. Woodruff got suspicious and started asking questions. He discovered that his father had persuaded all Woodruff's previous employers to sack him, in order to teach his son that just because his father was rich he shouldn't expect an easy life.

Woodruff was so angry that he left the job swearing he would never do business with his father again. He took a job at the White Motor Company as a salesman, where his natural talent led to a swift rise through the ranks. Woodruff's father must have been impressed with his son's performance, because he invited him to join the syndicate that was about to buy out Coca-Cola, offering him a substantial amount of stock at a good price, which Woodruff bought.

Woodruff soon became vice-president of White Motor Company, and was offered the presidency of Standard Oil. But at the same time, the board of Coca-Cola – which had suffered in the recession of 1921 – also asked him to become their president. It meant a substantial pay cut, but he was intrigued by the challenge. He asked for a salary increase, and five per cent of any annual increase in sales. His father refused. Eventually Woodruff junior insisted that he must be given free rein to run the company as he chose without interference ... especially from his father. His father conceded and Woodruff took the job. It was 1923 and he was just 33 years old.

Woodruff later explained that his shares in the ailing company had a lot to do with his decision to take the job: 'The only reason I took that job was to get back the money I had invested ... I figured that if I ever brought the price of the stock back to what I paid for it I would sell and get even. Then I'd go back to selling cars and trucks.'

But Woodruff never did go back to selling cars, despite the fact that he made back the price of his shares many times over. Woodruff was an immensely strong leader, known by his employees simply as 'The Boss'. He had an absolute belief in the product he was selling, and he stuck rigidly to his single product resisting all pressure to diversify, so that he managed to build Coca-Cola into an unprecedentedly strong brand. It was decades before he even agreed to introduce other soft drinks to the business, eventually launching brands such as Fanta and Sprite.

Woodruff was a salesman, and that was what the company needed. He was a capable manager, able to oversee an effective corporate structure and to maximise profits, and he had an excellent ability to spot and develop talented people. He had a powerful presence, and his employees would do anything to win his praise. He recognised that understated displays of power were the most effective (he once said, 'I give parties; I don't go to them'), and he was totally in control of his business. When asked how company policy was made he once replied, 'It's made wherever I am.'

But his real skill lay in selling his brand. The company used bottlers in a number of locations, and Woodruff insisted that they all comply with a set of standards that ensured every bottle of Coca-Cola bought anywhere would look and taste the same. Bottlers who failed to comply lost local advertising or were bought out by Coca-Cola.

Robert Woodruff ... on recruiting talent

If you can get somebody to do something better than you can do it yourself, it's always a good idea.

Woodruff summoned all his soda fountain salesmen to a meeting and told them they were all fired. He declared that Coca-Cola didn't need salesmen. However, they were all invited to come back the following day if they were interested in joining the new department he was forming. Next day, he rehired them all as 'servicemen', employed to offer a free advice and repair service. To mark a fresh start, each man was assigned a new territory.

Coca-Cola's advertising before Woodruff arrived had been very negative – defending the use of caffeine and explaining that it wasn't harmful. But Woodruff did away with all that. He introduced widespread positive advertising: 'The Pause that Refreshes' and 'Enjoy Thirst at Work or at Play'. He also used the new media to advertise, promoting the product on the radio and at the movies, and used movie stars to endorse it. He commissioned a series of advertisements from the artist Haddon Sundblom in 1931 depicting Santa Claus in Coca-Cola's trademark red and white colours. Until then Santa had often been dressed in green or blue, and was generally tall and thin. But thanks to Coca-Cola, he is now universally fat, jolly and dressed in red and white.

Woodruff was a constant fund of ideas for expanding the consumption and recognition of his product. He introduced the six-bottle carton, he put Coke into vending machines, he introduced the sale of Coca-Cola at filling stations. He stipulated that it must always be served ice-cold. He used market research to find out what customers liked about Coke so he could improve the training he gave his soda fountain staff.

But of course, Woodruff wanted Coca-Cola to be drunk all over the world, not just in the US. His policy for overseas expansion included investing in local employees, materials and machinery to set up bottling operations anywhere in the world, ensuring that the business brought jobs and money to the local economy. This created a feeling of goodwill towards Coca-Cola the moment it arrived. And Woodruff ensured that all Coca-Cola bottling, advertising and promotion was standardised around the world, so that any ad would look the same, and any bottle of coke would taste the same, from Bombay to Baltimore, from Edinburgh to Johannesburg.

Robert Woodruff … on aiming high

It is my desire that everyone in the world have a taste of Coca-Cola.

By the time World War II broke out, Coke was America's favourite soft drink. But the best was yet to come. When America went to war, Woodruff announced, 'We will see that every man in uniform gets a bottle of Coca-Cola for five cents, wherever he is and whatever it costs our company.' The military was delighted to have a ready supply of the refreshing drink, which also brought the soldiers a little taste of home. They co-operated fully. (What's more, thanks to Woodruff's tactic and some judicious lobbying, it earned Coca-Cola exemption from sugar rationing throughout the war.)

Woodruff then decided to ship out concentrated Coke, which could be made up at the army bases themselves. The men who ran the reconstituting plants were given the title Technical Officers. The exercise was a genuine morale booster for the troops, and of course highly profitable for Coca-Cola.

One of the effects of the war had been that Coca-Cola had set up 64 bottling plants around the world, on every continent but Antarctica, in order to supply the troops. This left Coca-Cola perfectly poised to bring Coke to every corner of the globe. The war had also fixed in the minds of GIs and their families that Coke was the ultimate all-American drink. And the GIs had introduced Coca-Cola to every country where they had been stationed from Iceland to Japan. Woodruff's offer of cheap Coke to the troops had been a magnificent coup.

Woodruff officially retired in 1955, at the age of 65. But he stayed on the finance committee for the next 30 years, with his own office in the company's Atlanta headquarters, and he effectively continued to rule the company. He appointed various presidents to run the business, but he was always in the background calling the shots. He died at the age of 95, by which time Coca-Cola consumption had increased from 6 million glasses a year in 1923 when he took over the company, to 50 million glasses a day.

INDEX